NO I ███████
TEAM DRAMA

Ending the Gossip, Cliques, & Other Crap That Damage Workplace Teams

NO MORE TEAM DRAMA

Ending the Gossip, Cliques, & Other Crap That Damage Workplace Teams

Inquiries regarding permission for use of the material contained in this book should be emailed to admin@joemull.com or addressed to:

> Joe Mull and Associates LLC
> 1006 Old Hills Rd.
> McKeesport, PA 15135

Printed in the United States of America

ISBN: 978-1717552280

Credits

Manuscript Editor	Bonnie Budzowski, Incredible Messages, incrediblemessages.com
Copy Editor	Meagan K. Welling
Design, art direction & production	Melissa Farr, Back Porch Creative, Frisco, TX info@BackPorchCreative.com

ABOUT THE AUTHOR

Joe Mull, M.Ed is the founder and president of Joe Mull & Associates, where he works with organizations that need their leaders to become better bosses. Joe designs and delivers captivating learning experiences that give leaders the skills and tools they need to navigate the people management challenges they face every day.

Joe has been a trainer for more than 20 years, having previously directed training in university, association, and healthcare settings. Prior to launching his own firm, Joe was head of learning and development for physician services at a *U.S. News & World Report's* Top 10 Hospital System. There, he directed learning strategy and implementation for more than 9,000 employees at over 500 locations.

His first book *Cure for the Common Leader: What Physicians and Managers Must Do to Engage and Inspire Healthcare Teams* has been called "one of the most practical healthcare leadership books you will ever read."

Joe is the publisher of the *Help for Healthcare Leaders* email newsletter and host of the instructional YouTube series *Your Practice Ain't Perfect*. He has taught leadership courses at Ohio University and the University of Pittsburgh and is a Professional member of the National Speakers Association. He holds a Bachelor of Arts degree from Indiana University of Pennsylvania and a Master's degree in Education from Ohio University. Joe resides in the suburbs of Pittsburgh, PA with his wife and 3 children.

This book is dedicated to those who selflessly support their teammates without ego or expectation, even when it's hard.

Table of Contents

INTRODUCTION

INTRODUCTION

"We have a race problem."

Annette was the office manager in a busy doctor's office. Situated in an economically distressed community, most of the patients and families who visited this primary care clinic had little formal education or income. The staff there faced numerous challenges in their roles and, most days, their clinic was a tough place to work.

Annette waited for me to process her proclamation. As I sat at the table between Annette and Nancy, the practice administrator, I waited for more. The two ladies briefly made eye contact with each other, then looked down at the table. Clearly, they were hesitant to talk about their struggles.

"Okay," I said slowly, after more than a few moments had passed. "Tell me what's happening here."

They locked eyes again, then Annette turned her gaze toward me. "Well," she started, "we have two groups here. The white girls and the black girls. And they are constantly at war with each other. There is drama every day. Every. Day."

"Can you give me some examples?" I inquired.

"They don't talk to each other. At all. Each group goes out of its way to avoid interacting with the other group. But it's worse than that. Way worse. They intentionally bump into and trip each other. When someone is celebrating a birthday, their group gets a cake and the other group isn't permitted to eat any. They knock stuff off of each other's desks when the desk's owner isn't around. When new hires come in, they are immediately absorbed by one group or the other and told how things are. Anyone who tries to bridge the divide between the groups is shunned. I just had someone quit who was really trying to build relationships with everyone. But she couldn't take it anymore."

"Tell him about the cart," Nancy prompted.

"Last week, I happened to be in the hallway when a girl from one group *accidentally* bumped into one of the girls from the other group. But she obviously did it on purpose."

"What did you do?" I asked.

"Nothing right then. To be honest, I didn't know what to say."

"How long has all this been going on?" I inquired.

Annette and Nancy looked at each other. "At least a year," Annette answered.

"Okay," I answered, taking a breath. "Let's start at the beginning."

For the next 30 minutes, I peppered them with questions. I asked about other incidents of disruptive behavior that had taken place on site. I pushed them to identify triggering events and root causes of dysfunction and disagreement. I asked detailed questions about how Annette responded to these incidents when they occurred. I gathered information about each of the employees there and the roles each one played in perpetuating the problems in the clinic.

Our conversation made one thing clear: Annette and Nancy were at their wits' end.

"How do you fix something like this?" Nancy asked in frustration. "Where does something like this come from? Where do we even start?"

"That's the bad news," I said. "It's complicated. Everything you've described is fixable, but it will take time and require a lot of change," I said. "But there is some good news. ..."

"What's that?" Nancy asked.

"Your problems have almost nothing at all to do with race."

ON DRAMA

This is a book about reducing team drama. It is about decreasing the frequency of things like gossip, cliques, in-fighting, and name-calling between employees at work. There is no simple, pithy way to define drama. I wish there were. I would love to be able to explain it to you in a singular sentence, one that would provide simple parameters or defined criteria that you could use to determine whether drama is present on your team.

But I can't, because it's just not that simple.

One of the most famous expressions in the history of the U.S. Supreme Court was used in 1964 by Justice Potter Stewart in a case about pornography. In *Jacobellis v. Ohio*, which revolved around determining what is and is not protected speech, Justice Potter acknowledged that attempting to categorize obscenities – a topic that is subjective and lacking in defined parameters – was nearly impossible to do. He famously wrote: "I shall not today attempt further to define the kinds of material I understand to be embraced within that shorthand description [...] but I know it when I see it."

I can say the same thing about team drama at work.

I know it when I see it.

I bet you do, too. You know it when you see it.

While we might struggle to define drama succinctly, I'm sure you can give voice to plenty of examples. So let us define drama this way. Let's take an inventory together and use that term to reference our catalog of experiences.

Where do we start? Well, the very title of this book references two types of drama: gossip and cliques. We've already mentioned in-fighting and name-calling. What other kinds of team drama take place where you work? What kinds of actions and reactions do you see and hear between people that you might unequivocally label as "drama?"

If you're like many of the managers and supervisors I work with in my training practice, then certainly behaviors like whispering about others, bickering, complaining, and short-tempered outbursts would make your list. So, too, would things like eye-rolling, scorekeeping, dirty looks, playing favorites, withholding information, and saying "That's your job, not mine."

Are there members of your team who pit one person against another? That's a type of team drama. Do inappropriate conversations take place at work that are about others, near customers, or are not respectful of sensitive subjects? That's team drama, too.

Do some on your team promote silos? Do some actively work to keep departments, specialties, or functional areas separate or at odds? Are there employees on your team who are abrasive in tone or unfriendly toward others? Have you witnessed bullying, grudges, or accusations of incompetence? These are all behaviors that, in most cases, can be defined as drama or as contributors to it.

What else? What types of drama transpire in your workplace that you find the most troubling or among the hardest to address? Write them in the margin of this book to contribute to your inventory and to our definition of the term. As time passes, keep adding to our list. Each time something occurs that you experience as a form of team drama, return to the margins of this book and add it to our list.

You'll know it when you see it.

In addition to defining drama, this book exists to explore and understand its causes. Drama shows up in the workplace for many reasons. Sometimes it occurs when team members aren't given the tools or support they need to rise above pressure or disagreements; or it unfolds when the stressors of the workplace interact with team members' competing priorities, deadlines, or resources. Sometimes drama appears simply as a result of wildly differing personalities between two people.

While all of these circumstances contribute, in some way, to the manifestation of drama in workplaces, the most common provocation is simpler. Most drama at work is borne out of someone reacting to how they feel they were treated by somebody else.

Let's say that again, for emphasis: *Most drama at work is borne out of someone reacting to how they feel they were treated by somebody else.*

As we will explore in greater depth in this book, that reaction often triggers a predictable pattern of flawed thoughts and behaviors that perpetuate drama. If those charged with leading teams don't know how to help their teams successfully navigate and resolve these reactions, or don't take steps to prevent them from occurring in the first place, then drama spreads.

What is the business case for decreasing drama? It's almost too complex to capture succinctly. As you move through this book, you'll encounter numerous examples of the harm that drama can inflict on a team or organization. Drama, in a word, is destructive.

Drama can derail even the most talented, dedicated workforce. At an organizational level, drama damages morale, productivity, engagement, and retention. It leads to customer complaints, lost revenue, and a talent exodus. Drama contributes to wasted time, higher turnover, and inefficient use of resources. It can badly damage a brand's reputation and a customer's experience.

Drama also sucks the life out of every manager it touches, monopolizing their time, draining their spirit, and derailing their ability to tackle larger issues related to process, performance, or policy. If you're like most of the leaders I work with, you are tired of your time, attention, and energy getting devoured by team drama.

THIS BOOK IS FOR YOU

This book is for anyone who wants to influence the performance, interactions, or morale of a workplace team. It is designed to be a refreshingly honest look at the people side of managing teams that goes well beyond the concept of "teambuilding." You will get clear strategies and tactics to dramatically improve the quality of interactions between employees in the workplace. This book is intended to function as a how-to guide on engineering a high-performing, close-knit work team that won't consistently get derailed by drama.

Now please note: When I say "no more team drama," I am not promising you the complete and total elimination of team drama, nor am I promising that drama will not occur again. Your employees are human, and for that reason, drama will always periodically occur. A certain amount of "low-grade" drama might even remain. If you are a team leader, dealing with small doses of team drama on a regular basis is part of the gig. Sorry. That's just the way it is. Accept that now or go do something else, because *some* drama just comes with the territory.

When I proclaim "no more team drama," I mean no more drama occurring at the level at which it consistently does harm to you, your team, or your organization. This book endeavors to give you the knowledge, strategies, and tactics you need to reduce drama to low-impact levels. It also is designed to help you help your teams navigate drama more successfully when it occurs, which simultaneously strengthens your team and prevents the proliferation of further drama.

The audience for this book is team leaders. When I say "team leader," I'm not just addressing the person in the official role of manager or supervisor, though this book will certainly prove useful if that's the role you fill on your team. I'm also talking to any member of a team who wants to influence the performance and cohesiveness of that team.

I recently heard a decorated basketball coach talk about how his championship teams were filled with players who weren't afraid to speak up and challenge each other. He described how his players did not leave the responsibility for leading and holding everyone to high standards to the coach alone. He said he knew he had a great team when he didn't have to do much talking in the huddle. Instead, the members of the team would challenge each other. "When I had guys holding each other accountable, saying 'Get your act together!' I knew I had a great team."

This book is for supervisors, yes, but it's also for team members who want to get active in the huddle. Non-supervisors often can influence the performance of a team and its individual members more directly than the team leader. Indeed, the impact of many of the ideas and actions put forth in this book will be supercharged if they are driven by members of the team, not just by the team's formally assigned leaders.

For this reason, there may be value in having every member of your team read this book.

As far as I'm concerned, your title doesn't matter. If you want to transform a group of employees into a band of collaborators committed to working hard, getting along, and wowing customers while dramatically decreasing the chances that drama will do your team harm, then this book is for you.

WHAT YOU WILL LEARN

There are four things teams have to get better at in order to avoid team drama: Courtesy, Camaraderie, Conflict, and Cause. These are the four C's of a no-drama workplace team.

Part 1 of this book is on Courtesy. In it, we will explore the ways team leaders must articulate, enforce, role model, and skill build an expectation of courtesy and respect in all interactions, between all members of the team. Why? Because the quality of the interactions that take place on a team are determined by what team leaders expect and permit.

Part 2 focuses on Camaraderie. Familiarity, connection, and bonds of belonging lead to higher levels of team performance. That's why this section details how to help the members of your team get to know each other beyond their job roles. This part of the book will also discuss how critical it is for team leaders to nurture a sense of belonging across the members of a team.

Part 3 dives into the issue of Conflict. We know that healthy conflict must occur regularly for teams to reach the highest levels of performance. This section of the book reveals how team leaders can disrupt the flawed thinking and destructive patterns of behavior that lead to unhealthy conflict.

Part 4 is about Cause. A common cause leads to interdependence and shared effort on a team. This section challenges team leaders to become better storytellers. Doing so makes it more likely that you will give your team a purpose so worthy of their time, effort, and attention, that they can't help but rise above petty issues and inconsequential disagreements.

When teams get better at these four things – Courtesy, Camaraderie, Conflict, and Cause – drama rarely flourishes. When team leaders are inattentive to one or all of these areas, drama reigns.

When I visit with leadership teams to deliver a *No More Team Drama* workshop, I am inevitably asked about which of the 4 C's is most important or whether there is a particular order in which they should be tackled or attended to.

You should know that, when it comes to organizing these four C's – Courtesy, Camaraderie, Conflict, and Cause – I strongly advocate for groups to start with Courtesy. It is the foundation upon which the other 3 C's are built. Courtesy holds everything else up. If the members of your team don't treat each other with courtesy and respect, then improvement in the other three areas becomes much, much harder. That's why I've always thought of this four C's model as existing on a pyramid and started presenting it that way in training sessions, like this:

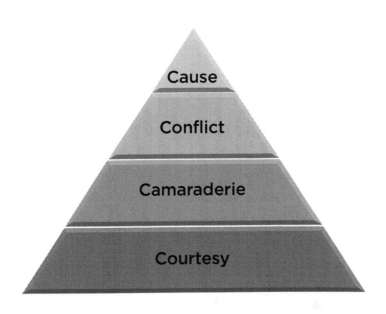

That isn't to say that once you establish Courtesy in your work setting you must progress up the pyramid in the order listed in the image. After making progress on Courtesy, you may decide that moving to Cause next is what is best for your team. Trust your instincts and do what you perceive to be in the best interests of the workgroup around you.

While I recommend consuming this book in the order in which it was written, I anticipate that many of you will revisit some sections more than others; your returns to the book dictated by the areas in which you need the most help.

As you make your way through the book, you will encounter a few things that are designed to enhance your journey and your learning experience.

First, there are jokes. Not many, but there are some. They likely will appear out of nowhere and be moderately funny at best. You're welcome.

You also will encounter, within each section, supplemental resources. There are four kinds of supplemental resources in each section, and they are noted with a unique icon as follows:

There are a handful of spots in the book when a visual resource might aid you in your learning. When you see this icon, you can jump on over to NoMoreTeamDrama.com to view the video content that accompanies that section.

In an effort to give you as much help as possible to reduce team drama, a downloadable digital toolkit has been created in tandem with this book. The toolkit contains a handful of activities and resources related to each of the four C's in the book. When you see this icon, there's a corresponding download available to you via the toolkit.

Learning requires context, which is why each section of the book includes a case study. These are in-depth examples of putting the strategies discussed in each section into action.

In each of the four main sections of the book, I have shared an additional piece of content called Advice from an Expert. When you encounter this icon, a subject matter expert will answer a specific question.

In addition to these supplemental resources, each of the four sections of the book will end with a summary of key takeaways and a bulleted list of actions to take to implement the learning and begin getting better results. These lists also can serve as helpful refreshers of content whenever you need to return to the book.

Before we dive into a more robust discussion of how to reduce team drama, you should know that, in most cases, the names of the people identified in this book have been changed to protect the innocent (and the foolish). Though names have been changed, every person mentioned, and every story told, is real.

Throughout the book, I will use a handful of words synonymously. I will use the terms civility, courtesy, and respect as synonyms. These are words that show up in workplaces across the globe but aren't always attached to specific behaviors. In some cases, they may be defined in internal corporate documents, but rarely are they translated to the day-to-day interactions taking place between members of a team. As a result of using these terms in this way, I also will use the terms uncivil, discourteous, and disrespectful interchangeably. While experts in communication and civility may rightfully debate the uniqueness of each of these terms, I choose to use them in this way to help make the absorption and application of the content of this book as simple as possible.

Along those lines, I cannot allow us to go any further without taking a moment to differentiate between drama and workplace violence. Often, discussion of incivility on the job results in an examination of behaviors that aren't actually discourteous but rather are forms of workplace violence. Screaming, threats, bullying, throwing things, physical intimidation, and discrimination are not forms of drama. They are forms of harassment, which is against the law. To label them simply as discourteous or as forms of "drama" is to minimize their very-real impact. Labeling them in this way also increases our tolerance of harassment in the workplace, which, frankly, should not exist. These behaviors are abhorrent. They are forms of assault. They have no place in a professional work environment. They should be unacceptable anywhere.

This book is not about reducing workplace violence. It is about reducing drama, the far more common forms of disruptive or disrespectful behavior that leaders like you might regularly struggle to address when they occur. You may even find that some of these behaviors live in a kind of grey area that leads you to question whether challenging them is even appropriate. In the pages ahead, I'll do my best to give you the insight, strategies, and tactics you need to decrease damaging drama where you work.

It turns out that the primary care clinic with the "race problem" didn't actually have a race problem. They had a culture and accountability problem. The culture there was broken, and there was no accountability for bad behavior. It didn't take me long to discover that the manager on site went out of her way to avoid conflict and confrontation. She was intimidated by her direct reports and didn't have the tools or training necessary to be successful. She also didn't have the resolve. When given the chance to take on the problematic behavior occurring daily on her team, she quit. "I just don't have it in me," she told her boss.

When a new manager arrived, the environment in that clinic actually turned around fairly quickly. The new leader had the will to affect change and the insight to know how to go about it.

If drama is taking place where you work, you also will need to summon the resolve to affect change. If you have the resolve, then the tool you hold in your hands right now is the only other thing you will need to get your team pointed in the right direction.

Let's get started.

PART I

COURTESY

The quality of interactions on a team is determined by what team leaders expect and permit.

COURTESY

The Pittsburgh Steelers came into week 15 of the 2015 NFL season jockeying for a playoff spot. With just two games remaining in the season, they faced a must-win game against the Denver Broncos in Denver's home stadium. Lose, and Pittsburgh's chances of making the post-season tournament were slim. A playoff atmosphere greeted both teams on a cold December day in Mile High stadium.

The first half of the game was a defensive nightmare for the Steelers. While their offense managed to grind out 10 points, they couldn't stop the Broncos from scoring. Time and again, led by a back-up quarterback, the Broncos took the field, moved the ball, and added points to the scoreboard. With just a few minutes remaining in the first half, the Steelers were down 27 to 10, their entire season in jeopardy. Members of the defense were seen on the sideline barking at each other after each on-the-field failure.

Prior to the game, an NFL Films crew had mic'd up Pittsburgh head coach Mike Tomlin, documenting his interactions on the sideline throughout the game. After the Broncos scored another touchdown, shredding the Steelers defense, starting safety Mike Mitchell was captured venting his frustration to Coach Tomlin about how his teammates were performing.

"We gotta get on the same page! They're not beating us; we're beating ourselves!" he implored.

"Ok," Coach Tomlin calmly replied. "But what we can't do is get frustrated and stop talking to each other."

A short time later, Coach Tomlin gathered his defensive backs, again reminding them to work together. "Keep everyone cool," he said. "Keep everyone communicating."

 You can access the NFL Films clip featuring these exchanges by visiting **NoMoreTeamDrama.com**.

At a pivotal moment for the team, a moment when everyone was in a heightened state of stress and agitation, his advice and feedback focused on the kinds of exchanges taking place between members of the team. In that moment, many leaders would have focused on strategy or execution. They would have focused on the technical application of the performance (what is referred to in football parlance as "X's and O's"). Instead, he reminded those in his charge how important it is that they not take their stress out on one another.

Coach Tomlin knew then what many seasoned leaders ultimately discover: that the quality of interactions that take place on a team directly influences the performance of that team in a multitude of ways.

WHY COURTESY MATTERS

Most people's jobs are hard. They may not be hard every day, and some jobs are harder than others, but it's reasonable to suggest that everybody's job, at times, poses some degree of challenge or stress or difficulty.

When the going gets tough, do members of your team take their stress out on each other? Do they raise their voices or adopt a snotty tone when tired? Do they whisper in corners about others, assume bad intentions among co-workers, or stop communicating altogether? These are the disruptive and disrespectful behaviors that fuel drama in the workplace. Sadly, they are common reactions to workplace stress.

Some teams, though, possess the insight and skills necessary to channel that stress in a different way. Some teams avoid retreating into these behaviors because they have become committed to treating each other with courtesy and respect at all times, no matter what.

If you, as a team leader, have not nurtured a set of expectations – ground rules for interaction on good days and bad – it is likely that the members of your team react to stress and to each other in unhealthy ways. Team members instead slide into those common reactions listed above or other behaviors we might describe as discourteous or uncivil. These reactions create drama.

However, when team leaders make it clear that courtesy is an expectation and they support that expectation with messaging, training, and accountability, the interactions that take place on a team, even on highly stressful days, are decidedly different. They are healthier. They occur in such a way as to keep drama to a minimum.

In this section of the book, we will explore why leaders must compellingly advocate for a culture of courtesy and respect in all interactions across a team. We'll define what discourteous behavior looks like and how to address it, discuss how to remove those toxic employees who drive drama, and identify the tactics and behaviors team leaders must use to cultivate a culture of courtesy all year long.

The very foundation of a no-drama workplace team is the expectation of courtesy in all interactions. Team leaders have to start with courtesy and make progress in this area first, or nothing else advocated for in the other sections of this book is achievable.

Where do we start? With one undeniable team-building truth: The quality of interactions that take place on your team is determined by what you expect and permit.

DO YOU EXPECT RESPECT?

Do you expect members of your teams to treat each other with courtesy and respect in the workplace? If you are like most of the professionals I meet, you probably answer this question with an enthusiastic "Yes!" I often ask this question to audiences while keynoting conferences or in training workshops. I will ask, "How many of you expect everyone on your team to treat each other with courtesy and respect at all times?" Virtually every hand in the room goes up. "Of course we expect it!" you will tell me. If you are like most team leaders I meet, you are quite shocked when I tell you the truth.

No, you don't.

If you truly had this expectation – that members of your teams must treat each other with courtesy and respect at all times, no matter what – then discourteous and disrespectful behavior would be a rare sight on your team. If you legitimately set such an expectation – if you defined it, insisted on it, and worked tirelessly to make it a part of the culture there – then drama in all its forms would occur with less frequency.

When leaders and team members say "Of course we expect it!" what they actually mean is that they *hope* for it. They, like you, hope that a group of adults working together toward common goals would be able to communicate and collaborate in ways that are consistently devoid of discourteous or disrespectful behaviors.

Hope, sadly, is not an effective teambuilding strategy. Team leaders must state explicitly that members of the team are expected to treat each other with courtesy and respect at all times.

I know what you're thinking. *Do we really have to tell grown adults that they are expected to engage in courteous workplace interaction? Isn't that something that adults with even a basic education already understand and should be able to do?*

Not only do you have to tell them, but you have to tell them repeatedly. You have to campaign for it all year long. Furthermore – and this will come as a shock to many of you who carry the title of "manager" in your workplace – you have to teach the members of your teams when, where, and how to engage in courteous behavior at work. That's right. If you want a high-performing, cohesive team, you have to teach your employees skills related to communication and conflict resolution. Additionally, you must help employees see when and where they are most likely to fail at courtesy and why that failure will most certainly happen more than once. These are the actions leaders like you must take to truly establish and levy an expectation of courtesy and respect in the workplace. When these actions are absent, the only strategy being used to expect courtesy and respect is hope. And hope alone won't get you there.

Relying on hope alone fails to create the kind of culture that ensures healthy communication. It also ignores a variety of forces at work that can lead people to act out toward one another on the job. Unless you take continuous steps to articulate, demonstrate, and enforce an expectation of courtesy and respect, it doesn't exist. Then, drama occurs.

THE COST OF INCIVILITY

Research suggests that a lack of civility in the workplace comes at a hefty cost. A 2016 study by the Thunderbird School of Global Management at Arizona State University revealed that 63% of workers indicated they had been treated rudely in the workplace in the last month. This is up 13 points in the last 20 years. In another study recently published in the *Harvard Business Review*, surveys from a multitude of industries indicated that among workers who had been on the receiving end of incivility:

- ✦ 48% intentionally decreased their work effort.
- ✦ 47% intentionally decreased the time spent at work.
- ✦ 38% intentionally decreased the quality of their work.
- ✦ 80% lost work time worrying about the incident.
- ✦ 63% lost work time avoiding the offender.
- ✦ 66% said that their performance declined.
- ✦ 78% said that their commitment to the organization declined.

+ 12% said that they left their job because of the uncivil treatment.

+ 25% admitted to taking their frustration out on customers.

Discourteous or disrespectful behavior between employees hinders communication, productivity, morale, service quality, attendance, retention, and overall performance. You know this already. You probably see the impact of incivility every day. There's a pretty good chance you spend a disproportionate amount of time reacting to, intervening, and recovering from discourteous behavior, lessening the positive, broader impact you can have on the job, on any given day.

In my own work training front-line leaders, the costs of incivility are even more specific. As discord and frustration rises between co-workers, errors increase and effort decreases. Necessary work gets completed less quickly or is left to others. Trust between team members also suffers. When uncivil behaviors occur, it's the behavior itself that becomes the focus for the victimized employee. An employee who is distracted by the sting of disrespect is no longer bringing his or her full attention and effort to work and performs less collaboratively with those involved.

Additionally, customers and business partners can sense when tension is present in the workplace or between co-workers. "Our patients pick up on a vibe when we're not getting along," one healthcare manager told me. "Something is missing in the greeting and servicing of our patients."

DEFINING DISCOURTEOUS BEHAVIOR

As I've traveled the country teaching leaders how to be better bosses, I've collected dozens of examples of the minute behaviors that disrupt a culture of courtesy and respect. First among them are subtle behaviors related to body language and tone of voice. While facilitating a full-day LDI (leadership-development-intensive) for a rural hospital a few years ago, one front-line manager expressed specific annoyance at the facial expressions some members of the team deployed toward her and others. "Whenever I ask someone to do something just a little bit outside of his or her comfort zone or that's inconvenient, I hear lips smacking, see eyes rolling, or hear them sigh."

This is a reaction that has come up in virtually every training, coaching session, and conference presentation I've given. I've come to describe it as "smack-roll-sigh."

You've seen it, I'm sure, even if you didn't know there was a name for it. It's the physical demonstration, on someone's face, of their unhappiness with something someone else said or did. A person's affect – the observable manifestations of someone's thoughts and emotions – often ends up acting as a kind of micro-display of discourteous behavior. These are emotional reactions: unfiltered and lacking in any worry as to whether they will disturb or offend. This is a tiny, at times unnoticeable, behavior that, left unaddressed, seeds a culture of drama on a team.

Smack-roll-sigh isn't the only inconspicuous behavior that fuels team drama. A few years ago, I was facilitating a leadership development retreat for the executive team of a small outpatient clinic to help them identify ways to create a more engaging workplace for employees. Early in the day, I asked those in the room to start listing the specific employee behaviors they found troubling or wanted help navigating. The clinical manager immediately raised her hand and said, "I'm sick and tired of [high-pitched voice] 'cher-cher-cher-cher-cher!'"

"What's that?" I asked.

"I'll hold a staff meeting or team huddle," she said, "where I provide updates or go over information. Along the way, I'll ask for their ideas or try to draw out their concerns, and no one says anything. But as soon as the meeting ends and I get six steps down the hallway, nine out of the 10 girls gather in the corner, whispering, and all I hear is 'cher-cher-cher-cher-cher.'"

"Oh," I said. "You're talking about the meeting after the meeting."

"Exactly," she replied.

Team

Employees gathering in the corner to gossip about the manager, a customer, or a colleague does harm to a team in a variety of ways. I'm willing to bet that when this kind of behavior occurs in your workplace, you see and experience a whole host of consequences. In addition to making someone feel excluded or belittled, it fuels speculation about what is being said. It sets up a dynamic where some on the team are granted permission to speak in an unflattering way about another member of the group. If you want to commit to creating an environment where courtesy and respect are expected at all times, this behavior must be labeled as unhealthy.

 To see a clip of me describing and demonstrating "cher-cher-cher-cher-cher" and "smack-roll-sigh," visit **NoMoreTeamDrama.com**.

"Smack-roll-sigh" and "cher-cher-cher-cher-cher" are just two examples of the kinds of behaviors that show up, unchecked, in workplaces, and that lead to a deterioration of courtesy and respect between members of a team. Drawing on a number of research articles and industry publications, as well as my own experiences working with leaders and teams over many years, I've assembled a list of behaviors that undermine a culture of courtesy and respect. I call them DDBs – Disruptive and Disrespectful Behaviors:

- ✦ Gossiping
- ✦ Forming cliques
- ✦ Swearing
- ✦ Snapping at someone
- ✦ Excluding other team members
- ✦ Making insensitive comments about customers, leaders, or other employees
- ✦ Refusing to comply with policies or accepted standards of practice
- ✦ Saying "That's not my job."
- ✦ Talking down to someone

- ◆ Using negative non-verbal reactions like eye rolling, dismissive waves, etc.

- ◆ Failing to respond to a request for assistance

- ◆ Sending a disrespectful email or voicemail

- ◆ Withholding information out of spite

- ◆ Holding grudges

- ◆ Assigning an unmanageable or disproportionate workload

- ◆ Ignoring concerns that another expressed

- ◆ Interrupting or talking over someone

[handwritten margin note: One Up Others / Correcting]

What other DDBs do you see, hear, or experience in your workplace? If there are other behaviors that you would describe as lacking in courtesy and respect that aren't accounted for above, write them in the margin next to my list. Why? Because taking a total inventory of the specific ways incivility shows itself in your workplace is an important early step in nurturing a culture of courtesy and respect.

Why do these behaviors show themselves with such frequency on the job? For one, those who are victimized by these behaviors often don't know how to respond or intervene, so the incivility goes unaddressed entirely. In other cases, the recipient is victimized by someone who outranks them in title or authority.

In some cases, personnel tolerate the presence of these behaviors as part of a high-pressure or high-stakes culture. In fact, you might look at the list of behaviors above (and any you added) and suggest that these are things we have to live with, from time to time, in the workplace. You may even believe some of the behaviors listed are appropriate in specific circumstances (and maybe they are: For example, while swearing is listed, I would not describe muttering "Damn…" when realizing you won't be able to fulfill a customer order on time as incivility).

But leaders who want workplaces where drama is minimal refuse to accept these behaviors in their workplaces. They are seen as forms of workplace violence that erode the foundation of courtesy and respect necessary to build a high-performing, cohesive workplace team. If you don't believe me, take a moment to reflect on your own experiences with these kinds of behaviors.

Have you ever been on the receiving end of one of the behaviors on my list above? How did it make you feel in the moment? How did it impact the quality of your work, your ability to focus, and the effort or energy you brought to your work? How did it shape your opinion of the person engaging in the behavior? How did it influence your relationship with him or her?

How you react to experiencing disrespectful or discourteous behavior is determined by a whole host of factors. Your relationship with the person, your experience or seniority in your job, your emotional intelligence, your comfort with conflict, your self-esteem, your upbringing, and more will influence how you feel about what happened, what you do about it, and the impact it has on your performance at work. That said, there's a pretty good chance that the behavior you experienced triggered some kind of negative reaction, which impacted your performance in some way. This confirms what we already know: Discourteous and disrespectful behaviors negatively impact the performance of people and teams at work.

We also know that DDBs often lead to more of the same kind of behaviors. If you have ever experienced one or more of the DDBs listed above, ask yourself this question in follow-up:

Did being on the receiving end of a disruptive or disrespectful behavior ultimately result in *you* engaging in one of the discourteous behaviors listed above as well?

If you suffered disrespect at the hands of co-worker, you probably felt you were treated rudely. Did you complain to other co-workers (Gossiping)? Did you describe the offender in unflattering terms (Making insensitive comments…)? Were you less responsive or less accommodating in a subsequent interaction with him or her (Holding grudges)?

When we experience disrespectful behavior, we perceive that we have been wronged, which often leads us to engage in some of the very same behaviors from this list to cope or settle the score. In other words, disrespect perpetuates itself. Drama leads to more drama, creating a vicious cycle. While I'm certain you have been the recipient of one or more of the DDBs listed above, I'm also certain you have engaged, perhaps even unknowingly, in one or more of them as well.

Because disrespectful and discourteous behavior is often ignored, minimized, and perpetuated, it is hard to eliminate. Yet the presence of these behaviors will slowly, methodically fracture a team. In fact, the list above captures much of the very "drama" this book seeks to eradicate. Dysfunction, then, doesn't occur as a result of a single event or incident. Instead, the team experiences death by a thousand cuts, with trust, group cohesion, camaraderie, productivity, engagement, and employee initiative the biggest victims along the way. If you want to create a high-performing, close-knit, no-drama team, you must work to decrease the occurrence of these behaviors while simultaneously working to prevent their appearance in the first place. This takes time, effort, and a very specific set of tactics.

REMOVING TOXICITY

I get calls weekly from teams and organizations that express an interest in having me deliver a variety of retreat-style programs. In many cases, I'm asked to facilitate an all-staff retreat with a focus on "teambuilding." Since that word is vague and subjective, I ask a series of follow-up questions to better understand what's happening at the site and what kinds of goals my client has for the programming. It is during these conversations that I often hear about drama. Conflict, in-fighting, low morale, cliques, and frustration are commonly cited issues. Shortly after hearing about the specific challenges facing the team, I always ask the same question:

"Is there someone on your team who could leave today and never come back and the result would be a dramatic decrease in the issues that you are describing?"

Almost every single time I've asked this question, the answer has been yes.

Most people who will pick up and read this book will do so because they have experienced drama in the workplace previously or are suffering through it right now, in real time. If that's the case for you, I can say with near certainty that the drama occurring where you work is likely being created and exacerbated by one or two key players. These are your toxic employees, and they are drivers of drama. If you ever want to get to a place where you have a no-drama workplace team, these toxic employees must either change quickly or they must go. There are no other options. The first step is keying in on an important distinction as to the cause of the inappropriate behavior. Put simply, is it a question of skill or will?

If the toxic employee seems unable to communicate effectively, manage their emotions, or adjust their style and approach, it may be because they lack the knowledge or skills on how to do so. In these cases, training and coaching may provide a path to improvement. In circumstances where the issue is "skill," it is possible the problems can be fixed and the employee can start showing up in a way that aligns with your expectations of courtesy (thus reducing the ways that person fuels drama).

However, if the problems stem from a lack of will, that is, the employee sees nothing wrong with his or her behavior or indicates that "this is just how I am," there is virtually no chance of improvement. When employees lack the will to change, leaders must put that employee on a speedy path to separation.

Let's be clear: The shortest path to decreased drama on your team is the removal of toxic employees who create and thrive on drama.

If the quality of interactions on your team is being negatively influenced by a toxic presence, the first step to initiating change is a behavior-based feedback conversation that outlines the specific ways that employee is causing harm. Prior to this conversation, you will need to collect a list of the most concerning behaviors, including the details of when they occurred, who was involved, and what was said. In preparing for your one-on-one meeting with the employee, make sure you can present your concerns as specific behaviors, not as descriptive qualities. For example, confronting an employee about being "negative" at staff meetings won't bring clarity to the ways in which that employee is doing harm. Instead, you will need to identify those actions he or she takes that you would describe as negative. For example, be prepared to describe interrupting, rejecting or criticizing ideas, or whispering comments under her breath.

When you ultimately meet with the employee to give feedback, your objectives should be to 1) spell out the specific behavior change that is needed; 2) identify a date by which that change must clearly occur; and 3) identify what happens next if change does not occur. The following case study will walk you through the details of how such a conversation can unfold.

Case Study:
Having "The Talk" With a Toxic Employee

After keynoting a conference in Florida, I received an email from a hospital manager we'll call Laura. Laura detailed her struggles with an employee, "Brenda," whom she described as "VERY technically sound" but whose style and approach are toxic to the team. Here's just some of what Laura shared:

> *Brenda regularly points out the shortcomings of others. She seems to like drama, is heavily involved in office gossip, and leads cliques on the team. She expresses her dissatisfaction to others and to other departments, especially as it relates to management. She does not understand or agree with the "right-sizing" we recently went through and is unhappy with her pay (which I can do nothing about). She tells others in the hospital she may "quit" while simultaneously acting like she wants to run the show.*

What Laura describes is textbook behavior for a toxic employee. This person's conduct is cancerous to a team, and it's highly unlikely she will improve. That said, Laura still has to take the steps to make Brenda aware of her concerns and give her a chance to change. If (when) she doesn't, it will be easier to move her out of the organization.

I advised Laura to begin her next meeting with Brenda by letting her know that she was concerned about her because she seems unhappy at work. Succinctly describe the specific behaviors you see in just a sentence or two, I told her, and say "*… so I wanted to connect with you to better understand what's going on and see how we can fix it.*" Then, I told Laura, stop talking.

Initiating a conversation by pointing out concerning behavior will immediately make Brenda defensive. This approach – the "*I'm concerned about you*" strategy – is non-threatening and invites Brenda to set the context for the conversation.

Brenda may try to brush Laura off, or reply with a short, clipped answer. Laura needs to remain quiet and see if Brenda chimes back in. If that doesn't get a conversation going, Laura should restate her opening: "*Well, you seem quite unhappy at work lately, can you help me understand why?*"

Brenda may voluntarily share many of the concerns Laura already identified (pay, staff changes, etc.), or share additional issues of which Laura was not aware.

Whatever Brenda's concerns, Laura will have to help her sort through the things that have the potential to change and the things that don't. To demonstrate active listening, Laura should repeat back to Brenda her understanding of her concerns. Then, after identifying those concerns that aren't going to change, Laura should make clear to Brenda that she has a choice to make. I advised Laura to say something like this:

"So, you're frustrated by the lack of bonuses, the new staffing patterns, and the number of errors made by the front desk. Do I have that right?" (Wait for her to acknowledge.) "Ok. Well that last one we can definitely fix, and I'd like to hear your ideas on how to go about that. Our pay scales and staffing patterns aren't likely to change anytime soon, though, so you have to decide if that is something you can live with or not."

Again, I advised Laura to then stop talking and be okay with the silence that followed that statement. She needs to leave room for Brenda to reply.

What Laura ultimately wants is for Brenda to acknowledge what can and can't change. When this happens, Laura can then let Brenda know that, regardless of whether she chooses to stay or will be leaving soon on her own, her current behavior can't continue. That's when Laura must get hyper-specific about the behaviors she's concerned about. To start, Laura can ask a question like this:

"Are you aware of the incredible amount of influence you have here?"

This is a closed (yes or no) question, but it's designed to get Brenda's attention and get her thinking about the bigger picture. Through conversation, Laura should spell out the ways Brenda's actions damage morale and atmosphere and cost her in the eyes of her peers and leaders. Laura must be as specific as possible, using exact examples of conduct, phrases, body language, etc. After outlining her concerns, Laura should give Brenda a chance to acknowledge and respond. Simply asking *"What are your thoughts?"* can do just that.

Brenda may respond by disputing the details of what Laura describes, or try justifying the behavior by explaining her intent. In either case, Laura must keep the conversation future-focused, informing Brenda of the specific changes that need to be made. Throughout the entire conversation, Laura should listen intently and remain poised and kind, but firm and clear.

At some point in the conversation, it may be helpful for Laura to give Brenda permission to disagree with some of the decisions that have been made or with the ways some things run. Doing so may diffuse some of Brenda's frustration.

The next step is crucial. Laura needs to ask Brenda to commit to the new behaviors immediately even if she doesn't agree that they are necessary. This brings the conversation back to the choice before Brenda: Stay and improve, or plan to exit.

I advised Laura that she can trigger the end of the meeting by giving Brenda a specific direction:

> *"I'd like you to take a few days and think about whether you want a future here and whether you can succeed in the current environment. I'll follow up with you in a couple of days to get your thoughts."*

What's important to note here is that Laura's goal should not be to get Brenda to agree that her behavior is problematic. While that would be ideal, it's not likely to happen with toxic employees. Laura instead should make it clear that even if Brenda rejects the feedback, new behaviors are still expected.

In the aftermath of a meeting like this, two things are absolutely crucial. The first is a documented summary of the conversation that took place. Consult with your Human Resources team to identify the best and preferred way of doing this where you work. Often, sending the employee an email thanking them for the conversation and recapping what was said will suffice. The second critical step is a follow-up conversation. When Laura circles back to Brenda in a few days, she should ask her about her choice. If Brenda reverts back to voicing all her complaints, Laura should calmly state that, as they discussed before, the things she's frustrated by aren't likely to change and that Brenda needs to start showing up in the more positive ways they talked about or take steps to move on. Brenda should offer to help and support Laura with whatever decision she makes but reiterate that it is time to make that decision now. Regardless of her answer, Laura must again emphasize that the disruptive behavior can't continue and that, if it does, Brenda's choice of when and how to move on will be made for her.

Laura must document all of her conversations with Brenda at every step of the process. If Brenda is truly a toxic employee, Laura should bring Human Resources into the loop as early as possible so she is positioned to remove Brenda at the earliest opportunity if (when) Brenda doesn't change. This can be a long, arduous process, requiring Laura to be in constant communication with Brenda, HR, and any other key stakeholders who hold sway over whether Brenda can be removed.

Too often, leaders tolerate the problematic style and "attitude" of an employee when that person brings other valuable skills, expertise, or impact to the workplace. It's very common to hear a leader say "I have a great employee, but …" followed by a string of concerns about how that person creates drama.

This renders the preceding statement false. You do not have a great employee. You have someone who is technically competent. A "great employee" is the total package. By elevating some job skills or institutional knowledge above the very nature of the person and how they work with others, you are creating the conditions for a workplace impacted by drama.

High standards are the key to success in creating a culture of courtesy. If you are working with a teammate who cannot come to work most days with a modicum of warmth, good humor, and a positive attitude toward co-workers, why are they there? If they fail to work collaboratively with others or demonstrate the behaviors we've outlined as courteous and respectful, why is that tolerated?

If there is someone on your team whose very presence fuels the disruptive behavior outlined earlier in this chapter, they are doing harm, despite the positive impact they may have on the organization in other ways. When leaders allow such persons to remain, it's the team that suffers in silence. Your best employees, those folks who really are the total package, are being asked to function in an environment that harms their morale, their productivity, and their engagement. When toxic employees are allowed to stay or are perceived by others as being able to "get away with murder," your best employees stop trying and may ultimately start leaving. It's time for that person to go do something else. Care enough about your customers, your organization, and all who work there to commit to a higher standard, one that insists on courtesy and respect at all times and removes toxic personnel. Don't those you serve deserve better?

WHAT IF THE BOSS IS THE PROBLEM?

While many of us work with terrific leaders who selflessly serve their customers and teams, unfortunately, some of us must navigate issues with leaders who are themselves toxic. I regularly hear cringe-worthy stories of people in power whose style and approach cause considerable harm to team performance.

If an authority figure in the organization is showing up in a way that is damaging to your team, your culture, or the overall atmosphere of the workplace, it's costing you. And, truthfully, you don't need me to tell you how or why. You already know. In fact, you probably spend considerable time maneuvering around this person's disruptive behavior, while trying to shield and protect others from the worst of it.

We've all worked in places where those with power seem to get away with more because of their title or position. This power dynamic must be acknowledged because trying to improve the situation often comes down to your willingness to report it, or at the very least, try and have a conversation with the problematic person. And that can be risky. Some of you reading this might work up the courage to act, only to experience a backlash of some kind, whether it's being scolded … or worse.

Let me be clear about something. From time to time in your career as a leader, you are going to have to speak truth to power and stand up for yourself and others. To truly serve your team, you may have to draw a line in the sand, decide that some behaviors are unacceptable, and fight back, on behalf of your team, your clients, and yourself. This takes courage; it assumes risk, but it's often the difference between suffering in silence and affecting change. For more guidance on navigating abrasive leaders, review the "Advice from an Expert" box that accompanies this chapter.

Advice from an Expert: **What if the Toxic Person is Someone in Charge?**
by Bonnie Artman Fox

Typically, leaders who exhibit toxic or abrasive behavior such as public humiliation, explosive outbursts, or condescension have little or no awareness of the impact of their abrasive behaviors. While these leaders may appear confident, they have an underlying insecurity about their own competence. Their aggressive behavior is a defense against the threat of others perceiving them as incompetent and inadequate.

As an employee, your options of how to respond are limited. In reality, it's not your job to address an abrasive leader's behavior. Just as it's not the job of an abused child to confront her or his abuser, it is not your job to confront the abrasive leader. It is the parents' responsibility to intervene on behalf of their child and it's the responsibility of the supervisor of the abrasive leader to intervene on behalf of their employees. With this understanding, below are four options of how you can respond to an abrasive leader, along with related risks:

1. **Redirect** – In the face of abrasive behavior, calmly remind the leader that you are on their side and want them to be successful. This is a tactic that gives you some control, so you

respond instead of react out of emotion. If you have a rapport with this person, a bit of humor can also defuse tension. *Risk*: The abrasive leader might perceive your comments as disrespectful or belittling. You probably will have to continue enduring abrasive behavior because this response is not likely to reduce or eliminate the leader's abrasiveness.

2. **Confront** – In a private setting, tell the abrasive leader about the impact of their behavior in neutral terms. Avoid showing any emotion and stick to the facts about what happened. Reassure the leader of your commitment to doing your part to make them and the team successful. *Risk*: Because abrasive leaders lack insight into the impact of their behavior, direct confrontation is perceived as a threat to their competence. Confrontation may risk your job security, or their unacceptable conduct could escalate with you as the main target.

3. **Complain** – Go to your boss and/or HR Department with a written account of what happened. Stick to the facts so you are perceived as reasonable and rational. Make your intent about being helpful in order to prevent a PR disaster or legal event for your employer. The most ideal complaint modality is if your employer has a confidential hotline to voice complaints. *Risk*: Unless several complaints are received, you may be perceived as the problem, a troublemaker, or whiner. Encourage all who are affected by the abrasive leader to also submit complaints.

4. **Leave** – Consider the pros and cons of staying in your current role and the likelihood of your employer exerting pressure on the leader to change. Gauge your decision to stay or leave based on if your employer shows receptivity to your complaints and follows through with limits and consequences for further unacceptable conduct. *Risk*: Loss of current benefits, seniority, job proximity to home, childcare, and ability to make the same or better salary with another employer.

Taking a stand to confront unacceptable conduct takes courage and comes with risks. Before you decide on your response, consult with an expert who will help you decide on your best approach. If you are responsible for employees who are experiencing abrasive conduct, make an informed decision that protects both the well-being of your employees and supports your organizational mission.

Bonnie Artman Fox coaches leaders in the key behaviors and interpersonal skills needed to create a thriving, productive workplace. To learn more about Bonnie, visit bonnieartmanfox.com. ✳

CAMPAIGNING FOR COURTESY

Imagine yourself interviewing for your next job and hearing the hiring manager speak at length about the culture of courtesy and respect present in the workplace you hope to join. Imagine going to new hire orientation on your first day and hearing the Human Resources director wax poetic about how committed everyone in the organization is to a culture where employees treat each other with courtesy and respect at all times. Imagine, in your first few weeks on the job, hearing the CEO, senior vice presidents, and your on-site supervisor reinforcing the role that good citizenship plays in the workplace. Imagine encountering signage, training, coaching, and a constant drumbeat of the importance of civility during your first few months on the job. Imagine your co-workers and assigned mentor sincerely encouraging you to speak up should you ever encounter any behavior you perceive as discourteous or disrespectful. Imagine observing one employee respectfully confront a peer about a behavior they felt was inappropriate, then seeing that peer accept that feedback professionally while responding with humility to their co-worker's concerns.

How would that influence how you feel about your workplace? How would it affect your attitude, mindset, and behavior? How would it shape your responses to stress, anger, and irritation on the job?

Workplaces of all kinds are filled with a variety of stressors. Deadlines, workflows, and emotionally challenging situations are just a handful of the forces at work day in and day out. In the midst of so many triggers, co-workers can be hard on each other. And as time passes, and colleagues become more familiar with each other, they stop being polite. They fail to restrain their reactions and emotions. Without a foundational expectation of courtesy and respect, one that is championed, discussed, enforced, and role modeled, courtesy and respect are one of the first casualties of stress and strife.

Campaigning constantly for courtesy and respect in all interactions is essential to creating a no-drama workplace. The responsibility for messaging starts at the top in any organization but, by and large, it rests with the local workplace manager. The culture of a specific team and the quality of the interactions that take place on a team are a byproduct of what the direct supervisor expects and permits.

Leaders have a bully pulpit. What's important to the leader, positioned correctly, becomes important to the team. What the leader talks about incessantly is what the team will eventually attend to continuously. When it comes to promoting and nurturing courtesy, team leaders should identify a mantra to sell to the team, and then champion that mantra constantly, encouraging team members to adopt and live it day to day.

To help your team get better at courtesy, you may want to develop your own mantra, one that captures the kinds of interactions you desire among all members of the team. Involving the whole team in discussing and selecting that mantra can be a powerful way to jump-start change and create buy-in across the workforce. Not sure what kind of mantra makes sense for your group? Then feel free to use mine:

We will treat each other with courtesy and respect at all times, no matter what.

In a single sentence, this captures the expectation and paints a picture of what could be. The word "will" makes it clear that courteous and respectful interactions are required. The absence of courtesy and respect is non-negotiable.

Your mantra (or mine, if that's what you choose to use) is something you have to talk about every day. <u>Yes, every single day.</u> Whether you are a supervisor or an active member of a team who hopes to influence how people treat each other at work, your mantra is <u>what you insist on, talk about, ask for, challenge others to embrace, and deeply care about. You must advocate for it as if the very existence of everyone's jobs and your ability to serve your customers depends on it.</u>

You must expel considerable effort talking constantly about why the mantra matters, what employees get by committing to it, and all the ways it makes their lives better. You must bring it up in staff meetings, emails, one-on-one meetings, performance reviews, and while working alongside others. You must support it via signage, discussions, and onboarding. Your mantra has to live at the center of your hiring, firing, and decision-making at every level. Every single person on your team has to get sick and tired of hearing: "We will treat each other with courtesy and respect at all times, no matter what." If that starts happening, you're doing this right.

Team leaders must champion a mantra that insists on the presence of courtesy and respect in all interactions. Doing so is the difference between hoping people will communicate in ways that keep drama low and actually making it happen.

DRIVING COURTESY DAY-TO-DAY

While leaders and team members must actively campaign for the ideals of courtesy and respect in all interactions, that alone will not lead to the reduction of the uncivil behavior that can infect teams. Leaders also must describe in hyper-specific detail those behaviors that lead to quality interactions at all times.

If you want the members of your team to know how to live the ideals of courtesy and respect day-to-day, you will want to create an inventory of those behaviors that ensures courteous communication in the workplace. This is a project in which you should involve the whole team. Set aside time for a team discussion on what it means to treat each other with courtesy and respect at all times, no matter what. This is a conversation that will take time and require the facilitator (probably you, dear reader) to be prepared with thought-provoking questions (don't worry; I've got you covered). If you are leading this activity, you also will need to probe suggested ideas for more detail and specificity during the discussion. Along the way, be sure to capture all the answers generated by the group, refining and clarifying them throughout the dialogue.

 As part of the digital toolkit that accompanies this book, I've created a facilitator's guide for anyone wishing to take their team through such a conversation to define courteous and respectful behavior in the workplace. This activity can be completed in as little as 30 minutes. The result is a list of specific behaviors, curated by your team, that enhance civility at work. To download this activity, along with the rest of the toolkit, visit **NoMoreTeamDrama.com**.

What's important to focus on during this discussion is generating a list of DO's. These are actions to take, on a daily basis, that members of the group suggest as key to a courteous work environment. What tends to happen when this dialogue begins is that idea-generating skews toward a list of DON'Ts: *don't roll your eyes, don't talk about others, etc*. While this is an important part of the conversation, the list you are trying to make should zero in on behaviors to *start* using, rather than on actions to *stop*. Leaders and team members will have far greater success in changing behavior by advocating for positive behaviors that drive a culture of courtesy. By listing these proactive, future-focused behaviors, you are ultimately teaching participants how to function with a higher degree of civility, which doesn't happen by simply encouraging the elimination of troublesome tactics. Behaviors that function in this way and that are likely to show up on your team's list include:

- ✦ Say hello
- ✦ Make eye contact
- ✦ Smile
- ✦ Be on time

+ Be prepared for work

+ Return messages promptly

+ Be clear on what you can and can't deliver

+ Assume good intentions

+ Give someone your full attention when they are speaking to you

+ Give credit whenever possible

+ Regulate tone of voice and body language

+ Say "please" and "thank you"

+ Know your own hot buttons

+ Pitch in and help everyone

+ Apologize

Once teams define the respectful behaviors they desire, team leaders must promote these specific behaviors on a regular basis. All of the efforts to campaign for a culture of courtesy described above – repetition, signage, etc. – apply to promoting these specific behaviors as well. Stakeholders must talk about them regularly, incorporate them into feedback and coaching conversations, reinforce them with signage and training, and periodically revisit the list to determine progress and effectiveness. Perhaps most importantly, team leaders must hold themselves and others accountable. You must respectfully confront personnel when you see or hear about behavior that doesn't honor the list generated by the group. You must apologize when (not if, but when, because you are human) you fail and deploy one of those disruptive and disrespectful behaviors into the workplace. These can be uncomfortable conversations.

Often the success of a leader is determined by the number of uncomfortable conversations they are willing to have.

One other note about partnering with your team to get clear on how to ensure courtesy in your workplace: Generating the list should not be a stand-alone event. Gather teams a few times each year to review the list and ask, "How are we doing on this stuff?"

Will employees forget to use these behaviors? Of course. Will they periodically fail, letting their emotions get the better of them or prioritizing their own emotional reactions over the new standards of behavior set by the team? Absolutely. We're all human. What's important is to continue holding team members to these higher standards, coaching them through their missteps, and providing ongoing support for handling conflict productively when it arises. We'll talk more about this at length in Part 3 of this book, as teaching team members how to navigate conflict in a healthy way goes hand-in-hand with establishing a culture of courtesy and respect.

GETTING BETTER AT COURTESY

When the Pittsburgh Steelers trailed the Denver Broncos on that cold December day in 2015, the frustration and stress experienced by the players boiled over. Members of the team began taking their anger out on each other. At that moment, their leader knew that a conversation about strategy or tactics wouldn't solve the problem. Coach Tomlin instead chose to talk to his team about how they talk to each other. He insisted that, despite the difficulties they were facing, everyone needed to stay cool, work together, and keep communicating. Reminded of the need for a commitment to courtesy, even while under duress, the members of the team were able to more effectively identify problems and collaborate for a solution. In the second half of that game, the defense shut out the Broncos' offense, and the Steelers scored 24 unanswered points to win 34-27 and secure a playoff spot.

To create a culture where members of a team treat each other with courtesy and respect at all times, the members of those teams must constantly be exposed to how and why to do so. These messages need to be crisp, specific, and rooted in the everyday situations and emotions employees feel in the moment. This is key to creating a culture that people love working in, where they feel respected and supported. When leaders aren't clear about this expectation – that courtesy and respect is expected at all times and in all forms of communication – you get suffering.

Remember, the quality of interactions that take place on a team are determined by what members of that team expect and permit. Team leaders must articulate, model, enforce, and skill-build an expectation of courtesy and respect in all communication. Campaign for a culture with courtesy and respect at the center. Engage in a dialogue about what courtesy and respect mean to the members of your team and what the norms should be. Define the specific behaviors needed to create such a culture and remove anyone who is unable to meet this expectation. Don't rush this part. It is the foundation of a no-drama workplace. Get this right, and it makes everything else outlined in this book possible.

KEY TAKEAWAYS
on COURTESY for TEAM LEADERS

+ The quality of interactions on a team are determined by what leaders expect and permit.

+ A nurtured set of expectations – ground rules for interaction on good days and bad – prevents your team from lashing out in unhealthy ways.

+ Key to establishing that expectation is championing it all year long via messaging, training, and accountability.

+ Team leaders must state explicitly that members of the team are expected to treat each other with courtesy and respect at all times.

+ Discourteous or disrespectful behaviors (DDBs) hinder communication, productivity, morale, service quality, attendance, retention, and overall performance.

+ DDBs continue to occur because victims don't know how to respond or the behavior is ignored, minimized, and perpetuated.

+ Toxic employees must either change quickly or be removed.

+ Team leaders have to start with courtesy and make progress in this area first, or nothing else advocated for in this book is achievable.

KEY ACTION STEPS
on COURTESY for TEAM LEADERS

+ Take an inventory of the DDBs occurring where you work. Get clear on what you are trying to eliminate.

+ Start teaching your employees skills related to communication and conflict resolution.

+ If a toxic employee is present, determine if it's an issue of skill or will.

+ Have a focused, behavior-based feedback conversation with toxic employees to identify the change that is needed, the date by which that change must occur, and what happens if change doesn't come.

+ If the boss is the toxic presence, choose a strategy to redirect, confront, complain, or leave.

+ Campaign for your courtesy mantra, bringing it up in staff meetings, emails, one-on-one meetings, performance reviews, and while working alongside others.

+ Support courtesy via signage, discussions, and onboarding. Keep it at the center of your hiring, firing, and decision-making at every level.

+ Collaborate with your team to identify the actions they will take to ensure a courteous work environment. See toolkit download for facilitation guide.

+ Hold others accountable to established standards of conduct. Don't avoid uncomfortable conversations.

Remember, to access the tools and videos discussed in this section, visit **NoMoreTeamDrama.com**.

PART II

CAMARADERIE

Familiarity, connection, and bonds of belonging lead to higher levels of team performance.

CAMARADERIE

In 1934, Stanford sociologist Richard LaPiere was traveling through a tiny town with a young Asian couple, seeking a hotel for the night. He had been warned by others to expect a refusal of service at most hotels and restaurants because of the ethnicity of his traveling companions. During this time in our country's history, perceptions of Asians in the U.S. were quite bigoted.

On this trip, the group had no such issues. The hotel they ultimately chose granted them service quickly, and without incident.

For unrelated reasons, Mr. LaPiere ended up visiting the same hotel several months later. On a whim, he told the clerk that in a few weeks' time he would be traveling through town with "a very important Chinese gentleman" and asked if the hotel would accommodate them.

The clerk immediately and forcefully said: "No."

LaPiere was intrigued. When his companions had been in the hotel with him months earlier, they had received service without issue. Now, the very suggestion of them as patrons was met with resistance. He wondered what could explain this disconnect in behavior.

result, he did what any dedicated sociologist would do. He launched an exhaustive field study.

For the next two years, LaPiere crisscrossed the U.S. with two Chinese friends in tow, seeking service at 251 restaurants and hotels. LaPiere took meticulous notes, recording reactions and logging minute details about every interaction.

Six months after each visit, LaPiere then sent a letter to each business that had been visited, asking if they would serve his Chinese companions as patrons at their business.

Ninety percent of those who responded said: "No."

Take a guess at how many times LaPiere and his companions were actually refused service during their travels.

Across 251 total attempts – 184 restaurant visits and 67 hotel visits – the threesome was refused service a total of one time for reasons unrelated to the race of LaPiere's companions.

LaPiere's study has inspired decades of research that reinforces a startling truth: The closer we get to another person's humanity, the more flexible, tolerant, and accepting we become. This is a concept some researchers refer to as *distance*. Understanding this concept is key to building a high-performing, close knit, no-drama workplace team.

WHY CAMARADERIE MATTERS

The Oxford Dictionary defines camaraderie as "mutual trust and friendliness among people who spend a lot of time together." By the time you read this book, you will have participated on a number of teams during the course of your life. Our jobs, sports teams, clubs in school, committees at church, and more are all different kinds of team experiences. If you've experienced camaraderie on a team, then you know how impactful it can be on the performance of the team, the effort individual members of the team deploy, and the overall experience for everyone involved.

If you have had the chance to work on a team where camaraderie was plentiful, you probably rave about that experience. Likewise, if you worked in places where camaraderie was low, it's likely you recall problems and suffering. Or, at a minimum, you experienced a kind of void in the quality of your employee experience. "The job is fine," you might have said. "It's a job."

When a sense of camaraderie exists on a team, employees feel pride, loyalty, and belonging within the group. These are core components of employee engagement – the emotional and psychological commitment to the job that results in more effort, better performance, reduced turnover, and higher quality. You also get less drama.

Teams in the workplace spend as much, if not more, time with their co-workers than they do with their own families. Drama thrives in environments where relationships are weak or transactional and where stress and anxiety are normal. To immunize our teams from a drama infection, team leaders have to devote themselves to cultivating camaraderie.

In this section of the book, we'll explore the psychology behind relationship building in the workplace and get clear on the exact kinds of events, interactions, and gatherings that lead to camaraderie. We also will explore the responses that workplace stress triggers and what team leaders can do to create a more tolerant, more forgiving, more flexible workgroup that is less critical of each other. Lastly, we'll spotlight the kinds of messages and conversations team leaders must champion at work to bolster the bonds of belonging that ultimately increase camaraderie and decrease drama.

To develop camaraderie on a team, two things occur: a decrease in distance and an increase in belonging.

CLOSING THE DISTANCE

Richard LaPiere's experiment, and the wide body of research on *distance* published since, makes it clear that we regulate our behavior differently depending on the level of familiarity and respect we have for a person. If you have convinced yourself that you treat everyone "the same" or that you treat everyone – to borrow a phrase from the first part of this book – with courtesy and respect at all times, you are wrong.

And I can prove it to you.

Imagine you are driving home from work. After a long, stressful day and a challenging commute, you find yourself just a few miles from home. At a four-way stop sign, you patiently wait for your turn to proceed. After everyone else turns or crosses the intersection, it's your turn, and you begin to enter the crossing. At the same moment that you accelerate, the car at the stop sign on your right whips into a turn directly in front of you, forcing you to slam on the brakes to avoid clipping their bumper. You bang on your horn, gesticulating intensely at the driver who cut you off. You. Are. Mad.

As you proceed through the intersection, fuming, you find yourself following the person who cut you off. You can't make out his or her face, but you see them look back at you in their rear-view mirror. You're still quite angry, so you throw your hands up in a "*What was THAT?!*" motion. Maybe you are so mad that you yell or point or keep chattering away. A few of you might even forcefully deploy an internationally recognizable hand gesture that features one finger in the middle of your hand. And some of you may even hold it there for a bit, to make *certain* the other driver sees it.

Then, at the next stop sign, the offending car in front of you turns left. As the driver makes his or her turn, you glance toward the driver's face, and they turn and glance at you. For just a moment, your eyes meet.

And staring back at you is the pastor of your church.

Or your child's kindergarten teacher.

Or the kind, elderly lady who lives a block over from you.

You recognize each other instantly.

How do you feel in this moment of recognition?

I present this scenario, with great humor, to audiences all over. When I ask those in attendance to describe how they might feel upon realizing they know the other driver, I typically get some combination of an embarrassed "Ooooooo…" or "Ouch!" Some describe feelings of discomfort or shame. One audience member told me she would be so embarrassed she would want to follow the other driver to his or her house to explain that she was *actually* angry at the guy *behind* her! (Please don't follow another driver home. It's creepy.)

Recognize what happened here. When the other driver was a nameless, faceless unknown, someone with whom you had no relationship at all, it was easy to unload anger and judgment at that person. This happens every day in a variety of settings, most notably on the internet. Don't believe me? Take just a few minutes to read the comments on political Facebook posts or at the bottom of newspaper columns. The vitriol, judgment, and disdain that strangers unleash upon one another can be startling.

(On second thought, don't spend a lot of time reading those comments. You'll be happier.)

In our driving scenario above, when the person suddenly became known to you, you regretted your behavior. Had you known that the person who cut you off and who you followed and gestured wildly at was your pastor or neighbor, you would have reacted differently. In other words, the *distance* between you and the pastor is shorter than the *distance* between you and a stranger, compelling you to more carefully and respectfully control your behavior.

A relationship exists between our familiarity with someone and the degree to which we regulate our behavior in that person's presence. In LaPiere's experiment, the clerks were less openly bigoted and more accommodating when the Asian guests were standing in front of them than they were when asked about them over the phone. Similarly, you had a less judgmental reaction during our imagined scenario to the driver who cut you off when you knew them.

When reacting to someone with whom we have no relationship or familiarity at all, we let the devil on our shoulder dictate our reaction. However, when we are in front of an actual person or we have even a passing relationship with that person, we hold ourselves accountable to his or her opinion of us in a different way and regulate our behavior accordingly.

If you want the members of your team to more carefully regulate their behavior with one another, you must work to decrease the distance between them. Otherwise, they too will listen to the devil on their shoulder, and react with the basest of emotions and selfishness, unconcerned with the reactions or opinions of others. You can see the recipe for drama here, right?

Team leaders can close the distance between team members by nurturing camaraderie. The simplest method for fostering camaraderie among teammates is to create opportunities at *work* for teammates to get to know each other *beyond the tasks and responsibilities of their individual jobs.*

When we connect with another person at work around non-work subjects – likes and dislikes, hobbies and habits, details about kids or grandkids – we find things in common, form stronger bonds of mutual trust and friendliness, and have higher quality interactions at work. These higher-quality interactions allow us to access the full scope of the other person's humanness. As a result, *distance* decreases and the regulation of behavior simultaneously increases. Why? Because camaraderie leads me to care about my co-worker *and* to care about my co-worker's opinions of me.

More regulated behavior between team members will lead to less drama. The tricky part is identifying effective methods for fostering camaraderie amid the busy day-to-day demands of the work itself.

TAKING TIME FOR TEAMBUILDING

Opportunities to socialize and connect are common on teams where cohesion is strong. There's a reason many teams assemble for potluck lunches; plan and attend company picnics; and hold parties to celebrate birthdays, babies, and impending marriages. These are simple, low-risk ways for colleagues to come together and shed the stress and demands of shared work for short periods of time. These kinds of gatherings tend to be effective at fostering group cohesion and team spirit when they occur with regularity and when they compel participants to converse about things that have little to do with work.

If your team engages in these kinds of events just once or twice a year, or the interaction that unfolds there never ventures beyond work topics or job duties, then your efforts will have a limited impact. While they may serve as a momentary reprieve from stress, their influence on camaraderie is low.

If, however, you frequently engineer these kinds of ways for team members to interact, you can increase camaraderie over time. Obviously, the word "frequently" isn't well defined. I hesitate to put forth a suggestion that if teams interact in this way "X" number of times, you'll ensure an increase in camaraderie. Every team, every workplace, and every type of interaction is different. For that reason, there really is no hard and fast baseline to consider. But in this case, frequency certainly would accelerate impact. Four times a year is better than twice a year. And six times a year is better than four.

If pressed to give leaders and teams a guideline, I typically suggest trying for a monthly, non-work-related interaction that helps team members connect. Monthly interactions of this nature almost certainly will close the *distance* between members of the team and nurture camaraderie. These monthly opportunities don't have to be complex or time consuming. And they don't have to eat up a lot of planning time. Simply asking a group to go around the room before a meeting and share their favorite vacation spot, all-time favorite movie, or favorite childhood toy, works.

 For a list of Ten Time-Saver Teambuilders for Huddles or Meetings, visit **NoMoreTeamDrama.com** and download the resource kit.

My hope is that you are picking up on the key factor for ensuring an impact on camaraderie: Whatever you plan or do must compel interactions that help employees learn more about who their teammates are outside of work. Holding a summer picnic where everyone sits with their "best work friend" and talks about work does little to close the distance between co-workers. What can you do instead? Perhaps you encourage employees to bring their families, which may result in your kids playing with someone else's kids, which then leads to non-work interaction between co-workers. Or plan a few games where the winners earn a desirable prize, then configure teams of employees for the contest who otherwise wouldn't normally get to have extensive interaction.

It also is critically important to note that your efforts do not have to revolve around big, sophisticated events or gatherings. Anything that helps team members learn more about teammates' non-work life or interests will likely benefit camaraderie. For example, try setting up a blank "How I Spent My Summer Vacation" bulletin board in your break room and encourage employees to post pictures of their summer adventures. If your team is comprised of a lot of young families, you can do a "Back to School" board in the fall for first-day-of-school pictures or a "Season's Greetings" board during the holiday season that welcomes family cards or photos with Santa as well.

The best strategy is one of variety. Mix an occasional "big" teambuilder – those potlucks and picnics, for example – with short teambuilders at the beginning of meetings or team huddles. They key factor in planning is that each and every effort gives participants the chance to learn more about who their teammates are outside of work. When evaluating potential activities, let this be the litmus test to determine whether your ideas or current efforts are likely to bring your team closer together.

In fact, two of the most popular teambuilding ideas I hear from leaders fail this litmus test. As a result, they do very little to close the *distance* and build camaraderie.

I'm talking about Jeans Day and Happy Hour.

When I ask workshop participants to share the strategies they use to promote non-work-related interaction on their teams, inevitably someone mentions Jeans Day or Casual Friday. While I'm a big fan of both, neither of these special days acts as a trigger for non-work-related interaction, so they shouldn't be counted as teambuilding strategies.

Okay, sure, it's possible that one person asks another, "Hey, where'd you get those jeans?" which leads to a non-work conversation about shopping, clothes, fashion, etc. But that's probably not happening. To be clear, I'm not telling you to cancel Jeans Day at work. Please don't do that. I'll get angry letters from your people. Just recognize that things like Casual Friday aren't teambuilders because they don't typically compel non-work interaction and thus foster camaraderie. Special clothing-related days at work exist for far simpler reasons: because it's nice to get to wear jeans to work once in a while. People like it and look forward to it.

For the record, those alone are perfectly good reasons to have Jeans Day. So do it. Viva la Jeans Day.

Another "teambulding" example I often hear from leaders participating in my training workshops is Happy Hour. Since Prohibition ended, colleagues from every industry have routinely gathered at a local pub or sports bar to share a few drinks and blow off steam in the aftermath of a long day or stressful week. And while there's nothing wrong with an after-work gathering over a cold beer and some mozzarella sticks, leaders and team members should avoid counting Happy Hour as an effective teambuilding strategy.

For one reason, alcohol isn't always helpful at cultivating camaraderie. Think about it. Is gathering a group of tired or frustrated co-workers and giving them all a disinhibiting substance at the end of a long day together really a good idea? Or could it lead to … drama?

The other, more notable reason that Happy Hour doesn't count as a teambuilding strategy is that not everyone attends. While Happy Hour is appealing to some, it's not for everyone. Some people just aren't into bar time. Some people don't drink alcohol. Or they have long commutes, young families, or evening obligations to get to. And for some members of your team, spending 8, 9, even 10 hours a day together is just … enough. If you want to nurture camaraderie on a team, the majority of opportunities to get to know each other have to take place at work, during work hours. Yes, the occasional Saturday company picnic counts, but the bulk of your efforts must take place during the workday, making them consistently accessible for everyone on the team.

Again, let me be clear: I'm not advising you to shut down your team's post-work Happy Hour habits (see my note above about not wanting to receive angry letters). If a group from the office likes to gather after work, great. That's their prerogative. Just don't count it as a leadership strategy for helping foster group cohesion or team spirit. That doesn't always happen there and even if it does, not everyone participates.

One other point for clarity's sake: Creating opportunities at work for non-work social interaction is not about forcing team members to share information about their lives outside of work. I'm sure you are aware that not everyone on your team is comfortable with self-disclosure. Some employees make their lives an open book to co-workers while others set strong boundaries and share very little with those they call a colleague.

Everyone is different, and no individual on your team should be made to feel that he or she has to share or describe details they otherwise would prefer to keep to themselves. If you are facilitating a teambuilder, gathering, or event, your job is to create an opportunity for people to connect and share to whatever degree they are comfortable, not to push participants toward a discomforting level of information sharing. A team leader's best approach is to ask interesting but relatively mundane, conversational questions and to keep the behaviors required for participation relatively low in risk. And as a general rule, stay away from any subjects related to politics, money, religion, or sex.

Frankly, that last section is good advice for anyone in any workplace anywhere.

For more guidance on teambuilding with a diverse team, check out the "Advice from an Expert" box in this section, which reminds us that generational differences play a role in how team members respond to teambuilding efforts.

Advice from an Expert:
How Do Generational Differences Affect Camaraderie in the Workplace?
By Cara Silletto, MBA

As one of the first Millennials in the workplace, I have several battle scars from people making snap judgments about me. When I started my career in 2003, people assumed I was raised like they were, had parents like they had, and would think like they did, so when I missed their expectations it caused a lot of friction. They had no idea how different I was from the previous generations of workers who came before me.

My mom was raised in a home where children were to be seen, not heard. As a result, when she entered the workplace, she accepted the chain of command without question. But as she raised her two young girls, she swung the parenting pendulum the opposite way and made sure we each had a voice as children. She would constantly ask us for our opinions, so you can imagine my surprise when I entered the workforce with an egalitarian mindset – thinking everyone has a say – and was blindsided by the hierarchical atmosphere others expected me to follow. Older colleagues and managers felt I was "overstepping my bounds" when I gave an unsolicited opinion, while I considered it part of the value I brought to the team. I thought I was helping!

Generational misunderstandings like this happen every day and can cause teams to crumble if people make assumptions and do not take the time to get to know one another. How are team members supposed to understand someone else's perspective if they have no time to get to know each other? When team members learn where co-workers are coming from and why they think the way they do, they work together more successfully. That's why it is critical for organizations to create opportunities for staff, and new hires in particular, to learn more about their team members in order to build mutually respectful, genuine relationships.

What kind of opportunities work best? As Joe shared, different employees have varying levels of comfort with socializing and self-disclosure at work, and certainly generational differences play a role. Baby Boomers tend to value privacy and prefer to keep work relationships professional, since many were taught to "leave personal stuff at the door." Meanwhile, Millennials and your youngest workers, Gen Z (born after 2000 and now entering the workforce), have "work friends." We will share almost anything with these colleagues whom we see in and out of the workplace. Gen Xers fall somewhere in the middle of that spectrum, depending upon their own perspective about privacy and workplace relationships.

But I caution you, before you start putting your team members into buckets by birth year, keep in mind, it's not about birth year. It's about mindset. The way you were raised plays a much bigger role than the time and place you were raised. This is why some Millennials are considered "old souls." If they grew up in a military family, were raised by grandparents, and/or lived in a conservative town as a child, they were not raised like me, and they probably think and act more like previous generations.

Every generation is merely a product of the way they were raised, and with more diverse perspectives than ever before in our workplace today, there are many different views that can keep multi-generational teams from being great.

Don't assume. Get to know your colleagues from all generations!

Cara Silletto is the President and Chief Retention Officer of Crescendo Strategies, a firm committed to reducing unnecessary employee turnover and the author of "Staying Power: Why Your Employees Leave & How to Keep Them Longer." *Learn more about Cara at www.crescendostrategies.com.*

When employees have opportunities to get to know each other beyond their job roles, it directly impacts how team members help, support, and react to one another in the face of errors or when under duress. It really is a relatively simple formula: If I get to know you a little bit, I might start to like you a little bit, and if I like you a little bit, or find some things in common with you, I might respect you a bit more. If I respect you, then when a slip-up occurs, I am likely to be more forgiving and give you the benefit of the doubt. I'm more likely to say, "She's a good person having a bad day." I'm also less likely to take my stress out on you in the face of demands or pressure.

The specifics for teambuilding outlined above provide a simple checklist for determining whether a planned event or initiative will contribute to camaraderie:

+ Does your event or initiative prompt interactions that are unrelated to work, so people can get to know each other better?

+ Is the event or initiative taking place during work hours, so everyone can attend or participate?

Creating experiences at work that get teammates sharing and interacting about things other than work is key to building camaraderie. This is essentially "fun with a purpose," and it's a core strategy for overcoming some hard-wiring we each possess that leads us as individuals to assume the worse in others (more about that in Part 3). But it's not the only component required to further camaraderie. Low-risk get-togethers alone won't ensure camaraderie grows.

Because an increase in familiarity doesn't always lead to a decrease in drama.

WHEN MORE BECOMES LESS

The relationship between familiarity and regulated behavior is not simple cause and effect. While more familiarity (less *distance*) typically leads to more careful behavior, sometimes a high amount of familiarity over time leads to less regulated, less respectful behavior. I bet you've observed this between co-workers on teams.

As time passes and colleagues become more at ease with each other, some of the regulated behavior that was present early on fades away. Years of daily interaction can tear down the walls of courtesy and lead co-workers to, as the opening credits of the popular '90s MTV show "The Real World" famously said, "stop being polite and start getting real." While new employees tend to be on their best behavior as they have not yet formed relationships with other members of the team, long-time colleagues can stop making the calculated, restrained choices that preserve relationships. That's when drama appears.

You may be facing this very challenge right now. If you have a team that includes colleagues who have worked together for some time, any calling they once had to manage their actions and reactions in the interest of maintaining collegial relationships may be long gone.

This is why building a no-drama culture STARTS with courtesy and respect as outlined in Part 1 of this book. As teams become more familiar with each other, the basic expectation that team members treat each other with courtesy and respect at all times helps insulate teams from less regulated, harmful behavior. While an expectation of courtesy and respect coupled with efforts to close the distance between employees are keys to reducing drama on teams, they alone are not enough. You actually have to nurture yet another relationship dynamic that goes beyond familiarity, courtesy, and respect: You have to nurture a sense of belonging.

As with the concept of *distance*, the need to attend to *belonging* in the workplace is rooted in some compelling social science research.

Think back to your first date with your long-term partner or spouse. You were probably on your best behavior. You wanted to make a good impression, so you intentionally thought about how you might come across to this person. You gave him or her your full attention, listened carefully to what he or she said, and tried to contribute to enthralling conversation. In the early stages of your relationship, you were probably extra courteous and forgiving of any blunders or missteps. As months turned to years, these highly regulated behaviors likely diminished, replaced by a level of comfort that almost certainly led to less careful behavior. Yet the passage of time has not lessened your interest in preserving and maintaining the relationship.

With your partner, as your familiarity increased, and the regulation of your behavior decreased, a more sophisticated bond formed. Grounded in love and a commitment to one another, this bond resulted in both parties accepting each other, warts and all, and is built on mutual respect and admiration.

Don't panic. I'm not suggesting you find a way to have everyone on your team fall in love with each other. What I am suggesting is that high-performing teams do ultimately develop a deeper sense of belonging and caring between teammates. This bond is key to insulating your team from the natural erosion of tolerance that time and familiarity ultimately bring about. Understanding how to fan the flames of these kinds of bonds requires us to talk less about psychology and more about biology.

BELONGING, NOT LOVE, CONQUERS ALL

A few years ago, Liberty Mutual, an insurance company offering a variety of insurance products, launched a series of commercials promoting acts of kindness. In these "helping hands" TV spots, we see one person doing something nice or helpful for someone they don't know, which is witnessed by an onlooker. That bystander is then shown, in a different setting, doing something helpful for another stranger, which is again observed by someone else nearby. This chain reaction continues throughout the commercial while the voice over intones, "When people do the right thing, they call it responsibility." The spot ends with the tagline: "Responsibility. What's your policy?"

If you want to see the commercial I'm referencing, visit **NoMoreTeamDrama.com**.

According to a company spokesperson, the commercials generated an "overwhelmingly positive response from consumers." The company received letters, emails, and phone calls from people expressing how moved they were by the commercials. Viewers described feelings of warmth and compassion and being inspired to be a better person.

These reactions are no accident. In fact, quite a lot of biology is at play here. Research suggests that when we get unsolicited, needed help from someone, we get a little jolt of good feelings. The same thing occurs when we offer help to someone and it is warmly accepted. Furthermore, simply observing one person helping another can trigger that same momentary burst of warmth and happiness. What's happening in each of these moments isn't psychological, it's physiological. It's our body's biology doing exactly what it was designed to do. That jolt of good feelings is the body's release of the hormone oxytocin.

Oxytocin is commonly referred to as the "love" hormone. Any time you experience feelings of love, friendship, or trust, that's oxytocin. It is also the chemical responsible for empathy. Oxytocin is there to help us survive. As humans, we are members of the animal kingdom, and like many other animals, we are not strong enough to survive alone. Many animals live and move in groups, which allows them to share the burden of survival, protection, and safety. Humans are designed in much the same way.

We are engineered to form bonds with others and feel good when we help or are helped by others. We are chemically incentivized to feel comfort when we belong to a group. This encourages us to form communities and villages and share burdens and responsibilities. Because we are safe and protected as part of a tribe, our brain is wired to release oxytocin when we feel a part of and protected by a group.

We get a shot of these good feelings when we feel secure in the presence of others. It's why we feel safe and comfortable among those who share our religious views or political beliefs. Oxytocin also is released with physical contact. Oxytocin is why we hug and high five. It's why athletes hold hands during stressful moments on the sideline.

We are chemically programmed to form bonds of trust and friendship, so we can collaboratively handle stress and challenges together. When oxytocin is released, we act as we were designed to.

Where oxytocin flows freely, people feel safe, feel a part of a tribe, and trust that they will be aided by others. In other words, when members of a team experience bursts of oxytocin, camaraderie develops. This is critically important in the workplace because of the active presence of another hormone on a daily basis: cortisol.

THE DRAMA HORMONE

Picture the most difficult person you've ever worked with. Are they a former boss? A current co-worker? Why were they difficult to work with? What did they do or say that was harmful or hurtful? Were they critical? Condescending? Pushy? Were you bullied? How did you feel when forced to work alongside this person? How did you feel at the end of each day? Right now, by asking you to picture this person in your mind's eye, a small cortisol response has been triggered. The knot in your gut when my questions forced you to revisit the thoughts and feelings this person elicited is caused by cortisol.

Cortisol is the stress hormone. It's designed to produce anxiety. It says "Alert! Alert! Be on guard! You are threatened!" Cortisol is the first level of our body's fight or flight response. It is released when we feel vulnerable, attacked, or alone. Animals get a shot of cortisol when they sense movement that might indicate a predator approaching. The hormone prompts them to flee to safety, then it dissipates.

While we as humans also possess this fight-or-flight response, unlike animals, we are capable of rational, analytical thought. We use our intellect to seek out the source or cause of our stress, to make sense of our feelings, and apply blame. Often, instead of fleeing to safety, our biased hard-wiring decides that the boss doesn't like us, or that our co-workers are lazy or out to get us. Because the threat involved is ongoing, the cortisol doesn't dissipate.

When cortisol is present in our systems, that is, when we feel stressed or threatened, it inhibits oxytocin. When threat or danger is detected, nature doesn't want us to trust or help others, or expect others to help us. Nature has one requirement: Protect thyself. So we defend ourselves. We say, "That's not my job." We seek the safety of our tribe in the form of gossip and whispering. We form cliques.

Think of all the forces acting on your team at work. Think of all the different ways this stress response can be triggered on any given day. It's almost overwhelming. If we don't create opportunities for our teams to form bonds of trust and reliance with one another, we endure a culture of cortisol, dominated by self-protective behavior. We place blame, see ourselves as victims, and see others as persecutors. We drive drama.

I've seen this play out, first-hand, in a variety of professional settings.

 ## Case Study:
When Camaraderie is Absent, Customers Become the Enemy

While working for a large academic medical center several years ago, I was asked to facilitate a staff development program for a group of employees working in an outpatient clinic. We assembled that day in a long hallway where I had prepared a series of exercises to draw out the challenges the team faced, which would then pivot to a conversation of how to overcome them and why they should try (because … patients!). In my two decades as a trainer, I have never encountered an angrier, more disgruntled group of caregivers.

This team spent all of our time unloading a steady stream of vitriol at the patients they see every day. "They all lie," they said. "They don't know anything about their insurance. They're never on time. They take no responsibility for themselves. They complain and whine. They yell at us. They're ignorant," they insisted. When I challenged the group to understand the source of some of these patient behaviors or acknowledge that some of these things come with the territory while working in healthcare, they became enraged.

One medical assistant leaned into my face and said, "This sucks. I'm out," and stormed out. It was a stunning display of burnout and blaming, the likes of which I haven't seen since. While healthcare professionals across the country all endure ups and downs, they generally have a level of compassion and understanding for the patients and families they encounter. None of that was present here. These employees insisted they were victimized every day by a group of thoughtless, evil people who caused them unwarranted suffering.

I should have seen it coming. In the run-up to the program, the on-site supervisor had a laundry list of complaints about her employees' attitudes. However, when I arrived at the site, she announced that neither she nor her two other managers would be participating.

"This is just for the staff," she told me. She did stick around at the beginning to announce that I was there to help participants "get your act together." She popped in again near the end of the session just in time to hear the team demonizing the patients they serve and watch the angry MA walk out.

"I guess this didn't work then," she said before retreating to her office.

This is an example of cortisol left unchallenged. With no accountability from leadership, no dialogue or coaching to help team members navigate the cortisol-inducing situations that show themselves in the workplace, the team became infected with self-preservation and blaming. After years of leaders failing to nurture bonds across the team or prompt more critical and reflective thinking about the patients, the members of the team saw themselves only as victims.

Had this team experienced the release of positive social chemicals like oxytocin, they would have had more moments of collaboration and trust. They also would have been more capable of overcoming the periodic triggers to mistrust, fight, or flee that pop up over and over in any workplace. They may have eventually formed bonds of belonging that could have neutralized the obvious anger and mistrust that had taken over.

DEFINING TEAMWORK

To nurture deeper bonds of belonging on a team, team leaders must place team members into situations that trigger oxytocin releases.

Gatherings and events, such as the ones used to close the *distance* between team members, do this, especially if the group experiences laughter and joy together during these gatherings. But team leaders must do more to grow, solidify, and maintain those bonds over time. Relying on social interaction alone, while key to closing the distance and triggering some regulation of behavior, won't result in the more sophisticated bonds key to team cohesion over time.

Team leaders also must create team interactions that celebrate collaboration, evoke a sense of community, and spotlight the ways each person contributes to the success of the team to nurture camaraderie. These are experiences in the workplace that lead to the release of oxytocin.

Teambuilding has long been recognized as a key component of workplace success, and our bodies' physiological responses to oxytocin and cortisol help us understand why. The most effective teambuilding efforts nurture a sense of "we're all in this together" among the team. They compel members of the team to focus not on the differences between individuals or factions within the group but on successfully overcoming the group's collective challenges. This move, from a "me versus you" mentality to an "us versus our trials" mindset, triggers an oxytocin release, which then enhances the bonds of those on the team.

Team leaders can nudge this shift in mindset by talking often about what it means to be a "team" and about how important it is to support, help, and stick up for one's teammates. This is something that successful sports teams, and their coaches in particular, tend to do well.

I confess to being a bit of a sports junkie. Live sports are about the only television programming I watch, football and hockey especially. I listen to sports talk radio and read a variety of sports blogs and magazines. And, yes, I am one of those people who watches the NFL Draft on TV. The first couple of rounds, at least.

My favorite part of the NFL Draft is watching camaraderie play out in real time. Specifically, I'm talking about the Twitter scroll at the bottom of the screen that shows athletes responding to their team's draft selections. Next time the NFL Draft airs on television, take a few minutes to watch this scroll.

When a player gets selected by a team, wait just a few moments and you'll start to see tweets from that player's new teammates. These messages almost always welcome the new player to the team, celebrate that player's gifts and competitiveness, and express how excited the veteran player is at the chance to "get after it" with the new addition. What's remarkable to me is that, in most cases, the veteran player doesn't know the rookie. In fact, much of the time, they've never even met. Yet these athletes are so conditioned to foster a sense of team, they immediately embrace and celebrate their new teammates, moments after they've been chosen. While that new player will certainly have to prove his worth to the team and earn a spot on the roster, he is instantly surrounded by a unified group, most of whom will go out of their way to help the new recruit be successful.

Athletes show up in this way because they've been conditioned to do so. Years and years of playing sports at nearly every level, of hearing coaches rail on and on about being "one team," of being supported, challenged, and yes, loved, by teammates have conditioned this response.

The most effective team leaders engage in the same tactics. If you want team members to support each other, to "have each other's backs," and step up as a dedicated teammate without being asked, then you have to constantly sound a refrain of, "We're all in this together." You have to talk about team constantly, including what it means to be a good teammate or a bad teammate. You have to challenge members of the team to take responsibility for making the team strong and cohesive.

Professional athletes and coaches aren't the only ones who recognize the value in this kind of team-centered messaging. Leaders in the military have learned how important that same mindset is to keeping everyone focused … and alive.

A few years ago, I traveled to Lexington, Kentucky, to deliver a one-day leadership masterclass based on my book, "Cure for the Common Leader." The night before our program, I was invited to dinner with the CEO of one of the sponsoring organizations, a soft-spoken man in his late 40s named Chris Hickey. At the time, Chris had only been leading his organization for about a year. For the 25 years prior, he was serving in the U.S. Army. He retired with the rank of colonel.

Col. Hickey, it turns out, is a highly decorated U.S. Army Ranger-qualified officer with a master's degree from the School of Advanced Military Studies at Fort Leavenworth, where he served as a War College Fellow. In Iraq, he commanded hundreds of soldiers, whose primary missions were to battle a brutal insurgency and rebuild a crumbling infrastructure while working to close religious divides and prevent a civil war. The success of his unit, which was awarded two valorous unit citations, was covered by The Wall Street Journal, New Yorker magazine, the Washington Post, CNN, and featured on 60 Minutes.

Col. Hickey, as you can imagine, is quite impressive. He also knows a thing or two about leadership and teambuilding, which we spent more than 2 hours discussing over dinner.

"When I became a captain, in my 20s," he told me, "one of my commanding officers told me I needed to figure out my 'Command Philosophy.' He told me that if I was going to lead people, I needed to know what kind of approach I would take, because I'd have to implement it each time."

Thankfully, the U.S. Army develops their leaders throughout their careers, via years of additional schooling, unit rotations through combat training centers, and operational deployments. Col. Hickey also embraced self-study. "I read numerous books and articles on leadership, both military and civilian," he said. Well before assuming squadron command, he began crafting a philosophy that would reflect his views on leadership and the type of climate he wanted to create. "The philosophy was developed into me throughout my career, but the year before I took command was when I started to write it down and craft it into a coherent design."

At the dinner table that night, Col. Hickey smoothed out a white paper napkin and began to draw. For a full 2 minutes, he sketched in silence, turning the napkin one way and then another as he drew boxes, wrote labels, and connected arrows. In a matter of moments, he laid out, in simple terms, his approach as a leader, his expectations for junior leaders, and the kind of culture he nurtured everywhere he went.

In the center of the napkin was the word TEAMWORK.

I pointed to it. "How would you describe what teamwork is and how do you get everyone to commit to it?" I asked.

"It's saying 'yes' first," he replied. "When a teammate asks for help, the first answer always has to be 'yes.' Only then do you ask, 'What do you need?' In most places, it's the other way around. People ask 'What do you need?' first, then decide if they'll help. That's not teamwork."

Describing teamwork in this way is beautiful in its simplicity, isn't it? It captures how important it is for team members to commit to pitching in and helping each other. It ensures team members are paying less attention to who is assigned which job duties or keeping score on who is doing what or how much. "Eventually," Col. Hickey shared, "you no longer have to ask for help. As teams get tighter and more unified, it just happens."

We talked at length that night about building teams and what leaders must do to get everyone on a team rowing in the same direction. His answers were crisp and certain. His approach centered around that "us versus our challenges" mindset, which he always kept front and center for his soldiers. "I told them all the time," Col. Hickey simply stated, "we have to work as a team to keep us alive and get us all home."

When I sent Col. Hickey a final draft of this book and asked him to review this section to ensure that our conversation and his methods were accurately represented, he sent me the following note:

"Overall, I would tone down the focus on me and emphasize that I was a product of a system that develops leaders. We are bred as leaders to be humble and always focus on 'We' instead of 'I.' That is why I am uncomfortable with the accolades on me. Any success that I had was within the context of being a part of the team's success. My most prized awards are my unit awards, not my individual awards. Leadership is not on what I could accomplish personally, but on how I was able to influence my units to accomplish things that they thought were not possible. I don't consider myself remarkable compared to my peers, but well-trained and versed in leadership along with my peers."

Consider it noted, Colonel. Your response above serves as the perfect complement to the insights on teamwork described here. Thank you for your commitment to selfless leadership.

And thank you, sincerely, for your service.

BONDING AGENTS

Leaders also nurture bonds of camaraderie by challenging teams to pitch in and help each other out constantly. Creating systems that allow the members of the team to celebrate each other's contributions and support can go a long way to accelerating growth in this area. Teams all over the world have come up with colorful, simple ways to do this.

At one of my first jobs, my department director ended every weekly staff meeting with 5 minutes of time set aside for acknowledgements. She would toss a pile of scrap paper into the center of the table for us to record our "kudos." A kudo was what we called taking the time to thank someone else on the team who had pitched in or taken on something that was beyond the scope of their job. On the scraps of paper, we would write the name of the person we wanted to acknowledge and a one-sentence description of how they went above and beyond.

Each week, the director would collect these slips of paper and every 2-3 weeks she would pull one from a hat and award that person a gift or special privilege. The more you pitched in and helped your teammates, the more kudos you would receive. The more kudos someone received, the better their odds of winning "the prize." Of course, that had very little to do with why people participated. In the end, we all enjoyed the chance to publicly thank and celebrate our colleagues who stepped up week to week. By the second year of the program, there was no more pulling for prizes. Kudos become solely about acknowledging the help and support we received from others.

Variations of this system exist in workplaces of every kind. Some teams create mascots or trophies that get awarded to stand-out teammates by their peers or passed around the office on a weekly or monthly basis. Other teams use bulletin boards or notes on the lounge refrigerator. Whatever the method, the purpose behind these efforts is simple and clear: Giving members of teams the chance to acknowledge each other keeps "pitching in" in the spotlight, which affirms and reinforces the very behaviors we want to see on a team. It also releases oxytocin, which strengthens the bonds of camaraderie, keeping drama at bay.

Another way leaders create a culture of oxytocin and promote a "we're all in this together" mentality is by periodically holding team retreats. Done well, these kinds of events provide an opportunity for team members to talk to each other about how they work together. Often with the help of professional facilitation, a mix of fun, compelling activities can lead to a rich dialogue about what's working on a team and what can improve.

Not long ago, I witnessed a powerful moment at one such team retreat. While facilitating a staff development retreat for a team of approximately 20 professionals, a senior leader I'll call Brad spoke up, apologizing for his brusque nature. The activity taking place asked members of the team to identify things taking place at work they hoped would stop. While most answered with ideas about things other people could change, Brad said the change he'd most like to see was within himself. He acknowledged that too often he could snap at staff or give curt answers to questions. Brad said he was aware of the behavior, wasn't proud of it, and was working on it. Then, Brad noted how much he deeply cared about each person on the team and how truly appreciative he was for all their hard work. The response in the room was instantaneous and profound. Participants described being deeply grateful that this leader spoke up. Weeks later, participants were still talking about that moment. Brad's sincere sharing triggered an oxytocin release among everyone in attendance, which further enhanced the bonds between the members of the team.

The tactics outlined here – talking constantly about being a team, celebrating the unity of the team, encouraging members to spotlight others' contributions, and periodically gathering for more in-depth work and connection – trigger oxytocin releases which strengthen the bonds of camaraderie. These tactics are your bonding agents, as a team leader. They also counteract the cortisol that is regularly released via the stress of work.

It should be noted that there are certainly circumstances where a team leader could do everything outlined in this section and it would not result in an increase in camaraderie between members of a team. That's because, as with many kinds of relationships in life, sometimes things simply run their course. Simon left Garfunkel. Angelina left Brad. Taylor Swift left country music. Time passes. People change. Sometimes the best thing for everyone involved is to part ways and move on. Supporting a breakup might be your best course of action when it comes to enhancing camaraderie and reducing team drama.

GETTING BETTER AT CAMARADERIE

What we know about human psychology and biology creates a compelling case for why teams in the workplace must be given opportunities to form more familiar, more sophisticated relationships with one other. The result is a closing of the distance between team members, which can lead to more regulated behavior. And when team leaders also work to nurture bonds of belonging across the team, stronger relationships result across the team, increasing the chances that they can overcome anything together.

So find the fun at work. Gather and talk and laugh and learn about each other. Create opportunities to nurture deeper, more authentic connections between members of your team. The camaraderie that results acts as a kind of super-serum that inoculates the team from stress and drama.

KEY TAKEAWAYS
on CAMARADERIE for TEAM LEADERS

- ✦ Drama thrives in environments where relationships are weak or transactional and where stress and anxiety are normal.

- ✦ Familiarity, connection, and bonds of belonging lead to higher levels of team performance.

- ✦ The closer we get to another person's humanity, the more flexible, tolerant, and accepting we become.

- ✦ Camaraderie is a mutual trust and friendliness among people who spend a lot of time together.

- ✦ Teams develop camaraderie when two things occur: a decrease in *distance* and an increase in belonging.

- ✦ A high amount of familiarity over time can lead to less regulated, less respectful behavior.

- ✦ Bonds of belonging insulate your team from the natural erosion of tolerance that time and familiarity ultimately bring about.

- ✦ Everyday stress at work can trigger a fight-or-flight response that neutralizes collaboration, making camaraderie all the more important.

✦ Celebrating collaboration, evoking a sense of community, and spotlighting the ways each person contributes to the success of the team nurtures the deeper bonds of real camaraderie.

KEY ACTION STEPS
on CAMARADERIE for TEAM LEADERS

✦ Create opportunities for team members to get to know each other beyond the tasks and responsibilities of their jobs.

✦ Try for a monthly, non-work-related interaction that helps team members connect.

✦ Make sure teambuilding compels interaction that helps employees learn more about who their teammates are outside of work.

✦ Mix an occasional "big" teambuilder – those potlucks and picnics, for example – with short teambuilders at the beginning of meetings or team huddles.

✦ Concentrate teambuilding efforts on work days during work hours to ensure everyone participates.

✦ Talk constantly about being a team, what it means to be a good teammate or a bad teammate, and that "we're all in this together."

✦ Create systems that allow team members to celebrate the ways others help and support each other at work.

✦ Support a "breakup" if it's what's best for the team.

Remember, to access the tools and videos discussed in this section, visit **NoMoreTeamDrama.com.**

PART III

CONFLICT

Healthy conflict must occur regularly for teams to reach the highest levels of performance.

CONFLICT

When my son, Miles, was around 3 years old, he fell in love with the game hide-and-seek. He wanted to play every day, often at bedtime. Most evenings, right after brushing his teeth and just before story time, he would run up to me and, with unbridled enthusiasm, announce, "Daddy, I hide! You come find me!"

"Okay," I'd reply.

"Daddy, I hide in here," he would say, while pointing to the closet.

Miles wasn't very good at hide-and-seek.

One of my favorite memories is of the time when he decided to hide in his sister's room. After telling me that he would be hiding in there, I went down the hall and counted to 10.

"Ready or not, here I come!" I shouted.

"OKAY!" Miles yelled back.

I told you, Miles wasn't very good at hide-and-seek.

I pretended to look in all the other bedrooms, in the bathtub, and in the hall closet. I peered behind doors and curtains and under the beds, all the while wondering aloud where Miles could be. Eventually, I walked into his sister's room and found him instantly.

Miles was laying in the middle of the floor, with just a small, pink Disney Princesses pillow covering his face.

Did I mention that Miles wasn't very good at hide-and-seek?

Stifling my laughter, I pretended to look around the room for Miles. "Goodness, where could he be?" I said loudly, as Miles snickered, his little body shaking under the faces of Ariel and Cinderella.

"Wait a minute!" I exclaimed. "I think he's ... right ... here!"

I tore the pillow from his face as Miles squealed in delight. We laughed together as I told him about all of the places I had looked before finding him.

"I'm a good hider, aren't I, Daddy?" Miles beamed.

"You sure are, buddy. That was a tough one," I said, smiling.

If you have kids, this story probably brings back memories. It's likely that you have your own stories of your little ones hiding in plain sight. When I described Miles "hiding" under the pillow, you knew right away what was happening.

Miles believed that because he could not see me, I could not see him.

This is why 3-year-olds in general aren't very good at hide-and-seek. Developmentally, they are not yet able to orient themselves to another person's perspective. While Miles will outgrow this tendency as it relates to what he physically sees, what we know about how humans react to one another suggests that he won't outgrow it when it comes to orienting himself to another person's perspective emotionally or intellectually.

Social science research makes it clear that, as a grown adult, Miles will inaccurately interpret what others think, believe, feel, and want, and then react to those erroneous interpretations.

Adults, it turns out, aren't very good at some things either.

And when Miles is grown and goes to work, his flawed thinking and misinformed reacting will create unhealthy conflict in the workplace, sowing the seeds of team drama.

WHY CONFLICT MATTERS

True or False: Your team would be better off if you could eliminate conflict in the workplace.

If you answered False, you are correct. Conflict is integral to the growth and development of a team. Conflict, when healthy, draws out ideas, creates buy-in, and gives all members of the team a voice. Healthy conflict occurs around ideas, assumes good intentions, is in service to your cause (see Part 4), and all exchanges are rooted in courtesy and respect.

If you chose True, there's a chance you may be prioritizing harmony above team health. Team leaders who insist that they "don't want to rock the boat" – an expression I hear often – actually are creating an environment that leads to frustration, misdirected anger, and conflict that is not healthy. Unhealthy conflict occurs in the shadows, assumes malice about people, typically includes disruptive and disrespectful behaviors (DDBs), and often avoids direct discussion or honesty. When harmony is the primary objective, emotions get buried. Then they explode later, often in ways that are confusing, misunderstood, or that mask the original source of the problem.

To reduce team drama, team leaders must guide their teams toward the thinking and behaviors that lead to healthy conflict, and away from the actions and reactions of unhealthy conflict. This section of the book will equip you with insights into how to do just that.

We will pinpoint the flawed thinking your employees use daily when they evaluate others' behaviors and motives and identify tactics to disrupt it. We will identify the harmful patterns of behavior that occur during conflict and name ways to interrupt them. And we also will discuss how to help team members learn when, where, and how to navigate conflict in ways that will keep drama to a minimum.

Teaching your team to get better at conflict starts with helping your team members see that, on most days, they are moving through the world with their own pink Disney Princesses pillow over their faces.

'WHY CAN'T THEY ACT LIKE ADULTS?!'

I've been training and speaking on employee engagement and team performance for years. In workshops, retreats, and during conference keynotes, I often will detail the various forms of drama outlined in this book – talking behind peoples' backs, scorekeeping, ignoring co-workers, etc. – only to have an exasperated audience member exclaim: *"There are times I feel like I'm back in high school! Why can't my team just act like adults?!"*

Have you ever felt this way? I've found it's rare to encounter a team leader who hasn't had moments where they've thought, *"Are you kidding me?! This is juvenile behavior!"* when navigating the snotty, bratty behavior that team members can hurl at each other.

It turns out that your employees are acting like adults. Much of what we know about the human psyche makes it clear that in almost all we do, we are *egocentric*. As we move through the world, we absorb and process everything with ourselves at the center. Take, for example, an experience a former colleague of mine had at Wal-Mart.

Abdul is Palestinian. He grew up speaking Arabic. To this day, when he signs his name, he writes from right to left. Most of us in the Western world read and write from left to right. While checking out at Wal-Mart one day, Abdul swiped his credit card for his purchase, and when the signature box appeared, he signed, moving from right to left. "Hey," the young lady at the cash register exclaimed, "you write backwards!" The combination of Abdul's kind demeanor and dry sense of humor prompted him to simply smile and say, "No … you write backwards." Departing with a wink and a wave, Abdul left the young woman looking surprised and puzzled.

Or consider the classic joke about the man at the side of the river. Seeing another person across the water, he shouts over, "Hey! How do I get to the other side of the river?"

"You idiot!" the other man calls back, "you ARE on the other side of the river!"

We are, each of us, truly the center of our own universe. Because we are egocentric, we assign greater significance to our own beliefs, knowledge, and experience. And we distort the level of our own stress and suffering.

Here's a popular example from social science literature. Think of an important task you must complete in the next few weeks. This can be work-related or something personal. Write down the specific date you predict your task or project will be completed. Got it? Now, imagine that when you begin working on this task, that everything goes swimmingly. Imagine that there are no delays, no unexpected pitfalls, and that you are making speedy progress. Now what is your prediction for when this task or project will be completed? Write down this second date, which we will call the "best-case scenario" date. Lastly, imagine that you start your project and nothing is going well. Imagine that you get pulled into other things, that the task or project takes longer than expected, or that you procrastinated as long as possible. Now when do you predict this task or project will be completed? Write down this third date, which we will call the "worst-case scenario" date. It's the absolute latest date by which your to-do will be completed.

If I were to bet you and every other person reading this book that you will not complete your task or project by your worst-case scenario date, I would lose to a few, but the majority of you would be sending me checks.

This is an experiment that has been tested and studied repeatedly in social science research. It is called "The Planning Fallacy," and it's just one of the many ways we are short-sighted about our own abilities and efforts. The truth is, our ego leads us to habitually overestimate our strengths, capacities, and dedication. And we do it repeatedly, even in the face of convincing experience to the contrary. Have you ever budgeted time to complete a project during the weekend only to find it takes you 2 to 3 times longer than you planned? Of course. Everyone has. Yet, the next time you plan a similar project, you are likely to again underestimate how long it will take or how effective you will be at completing it.

This is one kind of unconscious bias you carry around with you every day. You are hard-wired to more favorably judge yourself than you should.

This distorted perspective doesn't stop with ourselves. Our perceptions of others are equally biased.

For the second time while reading this book, I must ask you to imagine you are driving home from work (I apologize for again putting you into another hypothetically frustrating situation behind the wheel). Imagine that you are stuck in traffic. A few yards ahead of you, the stoplight in the intersection cycles from red to green, then yellow, and back to red. You haven't moved. Time slowly ticks by as you stare at a sea of red brake lights. Finally, after what seems like an eternity, the first car in the intersection begins to move. Then the next, and then the next. Finally, space opens directly in front of you and it's your turn to begin creeping forward. All of a sudden, as you move your foot from the brake to the accelerator, a black four-door sedan comes darting up the shoulder to your right, whooshing past you as it kicks up dust and rocks. In an instant, it zips into the small space in front of you, forcing you to slam on your brakes. Never stopping, the sedan speeds through the intersection as the light turns from yellow to red leaving you stuck, once again, in almost the exact same place.

In that moment, how do you react? What do you think or say or do? Perhaps you pound the steering wheel or lay on the horn. Maybe you swear, call the driver of the sedan a name ("You idiot!") or give him or her that internationally recognizable hand gesture we mentioned in Part 2 as they speed away.

If you are like most people, you make a snap judgment about that person's character. You've deemed the driver selfish or unsafe. You assume malice.

What if I told you that seated next to the driver of that car was his wife, who is in labor, and they can see the baby's head? Or what if you learned that the driver was the mother of a small child who had been badly burned and she was rushing him to the hospital? Does this additional information change your judgment of that person's actions? Does it change your evaluation of their choices or character? Do you suddenly become incrementally more forgiving?

Most people say yes.

Here's the more important question: Do you recognize that in the absence of this information, you made up a story in your head about the character and intentions of the person driving the four-door sedan that was decidedly negative?

Social science research suggests this is something we do every single day. It even has a name: "The Fundamental Attribution Error." When someone at the office is late for work, what do you assume about them? Our minds tell us that the offending party acted irresponsibly. They didn't do what they needed to do, to be where they needed to be, when they needed to be there. They were being lazy or didn't try hard enough. We assume a character flaw or defect. Our minds rarely search for context to validate the behavior.

However, when we are late to work, we rarely judge ourselves harshly. We have a perfectly acceptable explanation for our tardiness, and we layer our rationale into our own self-image. "I'm a good person," we tell ourselves, often at an unconscious level. "I work hard and have a good reason for being late today." We have a much broader context with which to evaluate our own behavior. Yet, when someone else is late, we create an entirely different narrative.

Our egocentrism not only causes us to more favorably judge ourselves, it also leads us to more harshly judge others.

Stephen Covey, author of the renowned book, "The 7 Habits of Highly Effective People," once said, "We judge ourselves by our intentions, we judge others by their behaviors." In a single sentence, Covey eloquently captures egocentrism at work. When the driver of the sedan barreled past you, your reaction was based solely on behavior you found instantaneously appalling. Yet, you've probably been guilty of questionable decision-making behind the wheel. You've made choices while driving that were frustrating to others around you. Perhaps you've sneaked into a lane where there wasn't quite enough room to do so, or drove aggressively because someone you cared about was in trouble and that's all that mattered. In that moment, you justified your behavior, and in many cases, those around you would defend it if they had more information. Instead, the other drives, absent your justification, assumed malice. Some may have even given you that internationally recognizable hand gesture.

Here again we see egocentrism at work. We more favorably judge ourselves, in large part because we apply the context of our own values and intentions to the situation, which isn't something we do for others. At the same time, we more harshly judge others. Faced with only behavior to consider, in the absence of context, we make up a story that assumes bad intentions.

It is this naturally occurring psychological hard-wiring – more favorably judging ourselves and more harshly judging others – that employees bring with them into the workplace every single day. Now, add stress. Lack of time. Deadlines. Being understaffed. Small workspaces. Competing priorities. Fatigue. The nature of our flawed thinking coupled with so many corrosive forces frequently leads to workplace drama.

THE DRAMA TRIANGLE

At the core of almost all team drama is people reacting to how they perceive they were treated by others. Think about it. The gossip, cliques, disagreements, and other crap that unfolds at work, in most cases, can be traced back to someone feeling put off by something someone else said or did. Much of the time, the offended party is responding to their own evaluation of another person's thoughts, feelings, and behaviors.

What we know, however, is that our perceptions of others' motives and actions are horribly inaccurate. As we've established, we are hard-wired to misjudge people. This happens every day where you work. You do it. Your boss does it. The members of your teams do it as well. We, all of us, more favorably judge ourselves and more harshly judge others. Every day, we show up to work and assign inaccurate motives to others' behaviors. What happens next is the biggest driver of drama in any workplace.

We create drama triangles.

When a member of your team (Employee #1) is upset by something another member of your team (Employee #2) says or does, will Employee #1 go to Employee #2 to work things out? Does Employee #1 say to Employee #2, "Hey, this really bothered me and I think we should be able to talk about it calmly, objectively, and with open minds?"

Of course not. What does Employee #1 do instead?

That's right … they go to Another. Sometimes this person is a colleague. Employee #1 might say, "Can you believe that Employee #2 showed up 20 minutes late today and is still further behind on her part of the project than everybody else?"

The other person in this scenario, the person you've chosen as a confidant, looks around to see if anyone else is listening, then leans in to Employee #1 and says, "I know. I noticed that, too," and now both Employee #1 and Another are talking about Employee #2.

And the drama triangle has been created. Like this:

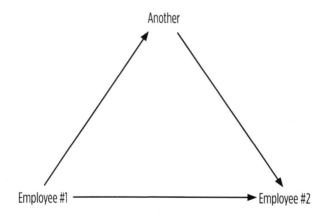

This is a pattern of behavior that unfolds every day in groups and teams everywhere. We do this at work. We do this in our neighborhoods and in our churches and across our social and professional networks. We even do this at home, within our own families. The last time you were irritated by something your mom said or did, did you go directly to your mom? No. You probably called your sister.

When we more favorably judge ourselves and more harshly judge others, we either stew about our (inaccurate) conclusions, leading to an explosion later, or we go talk to someone else about them. Think of all the drama that is triggered by this simple pattern of behavior. Gossip, cliques, paranoia, and more can all be traced back to this routine.

This pattern of behavior is actually a psychological model of interaction that was first introduced in 1968 by psychotherapist Stephen Karpman. He asserts that these are scripted roles we play across all aspects of our lives. In the drama triangle outline above, these roles have names: Victim, Rescuer, and Persecutor. These labels can be added to our illustration like this:

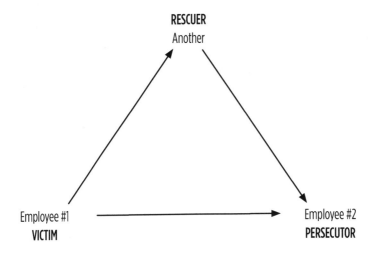

The Victim is the person who feels wronged. They say "Poor me!" or tap in to righteous indignation at someone else's actions. They seek out someone who will perpetuate their negative feelings.

The Rescuer is the enabler. He or she feels guilty if they don't help. But theirs is not an altruistic reaction. The Rescuer relishes being included and needed. Slipping into the role of Rescuer feeds the ego. They feel like a hero. When the Rescuer rescues, it affirms the Victim's perceptions of being victimized.

The Persecutor is the villain. In the eyes of the others in the triangle, they are the problem, the wrongdoer, the flawed catalyst doing harm.

Karpman asserts that not only do we play these roles regularly, but we also want to play them because they justify our own thoughts and actions. These roles are almost always a substitute for more genuine and adult emotions and responses. Instead of objectively evaluating our own reactions or more carefully considering others' motives, we slide into a pattern of behavior that reinforces the ways in which we more favorably judge ourselves and more harshly judge others.

Put simply: Drama triangles occur because it is much easier to seek out the comfort of validation than it is to step into the discomfort of confrontation.

I'm not just being cute or clever by labeling this pattern as a drama triangle. When Stephen Karpman published his work on this recurring pattern of human behavior in 1968, that's what he called it.

The Drama Triangle.

 How Drama Starts and Spreads in the Workplace. To watch a clip of me explaining how drama triangles form and flourish, visit **NoMoreTeamDrama.com.**

When this pattern of behavior occurs, it is a destructive response to conflict that inhibits real problem solving. It's destructive because the triangles don't stand alone. They eventually form a web of drama. Here's how.

Imagine if, in our scenario described earlier, Employee #2 gets wind of the fact that Employee #1 and Another are talking about him. How is he likely to respond?

He may confront Employee #1 and Another. This interaction is liable to be messy and negative. However it unfolds, suddenly the Persecutor in this scenario sees himself as a Victim. And if this confrontation takes place, the Rescuer now has grounds to see herself as a Victim as well. Drama triangles trigger more drama because no matter where you start on the triangle, Victim is where you end up.

The other response Employee #2 might have when hearing about the chatter between Employee #1 and Another is to seek out their own Rescuer. In fact, this is the most likely response in the workplace. If you heard that two of your colleagues were talking about you, it's very likely you would turn to a trusted confident, probably someone in your own circle at work, so you could vent. Your chosen Rescuer slides quickly and easily into their role, validating the disgust and dismay you express regarding your gossiping colleagues' behavior.

If your Rescuer, agreeing that "poor you" has been victimized, decides to go to the person in charge to complain about the gossip, perhaps she will get frustrated at the boss's lack of intervention. Suddenly, the boss is a Persecutor and the Rescuer has become a victim. The next day, the boss will remark to another on-site manager that she's fed up with her employees' inability to work out their differences. Now the boss is a Victim, and so on, and so on.

The egocentrism of each person involved – their unconditional bias that leads them to assume malice in others while simultaneously inflating their own suffering – leads to the formation of additional triangles, creating a web of drama. Like this:

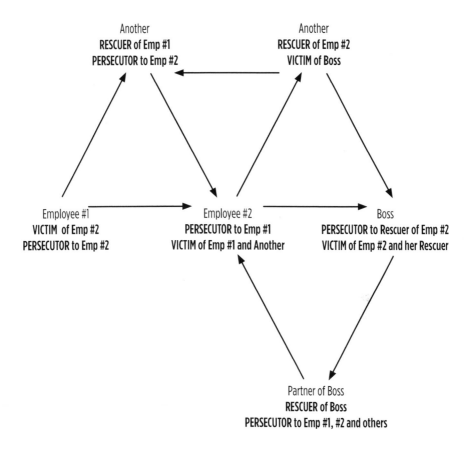

This is how drama is perpetuated in the workplace.

This also is the recipe for the formation of one of the most lethal forms of drama: cliques.

THE COST OF CLIQUES

You certainly know by now that, regardless of the setting, camaraderie occurs naturally and quickly between some members of a team. We've all had the experience of joining a group and quickly gravitating toward one or two members of that team. It's human nature. This doesn't always result in problematic team dynamics within a group. Sometimes teams are large enough that the formation of mini-teams within the group doesn't diminish a more global sense of camaraderie among everyone. However, because the pattern of behavior outlined above typically unfolds without disruption, cliques can form.

A clique is a small group of people with shared interests or other features in common, who spend time together and do not readily allow others to join. The first three phrases in that sentence aren't problematic in the workplace. It's the last phrase that truly defines a clique and the problems that cliques create: They do not readily allow others to join.

Cliques are harmful because, by their very nature, they end up *discouraging* camaraderie within a group. Mutual trust and friendliness – those core components of camaraderie outlined in Part 2 – are withheld from those outside the faction. As cliques take hold within a workgroup, those inside the clique can be victimized by groupthink and a herd mentality. They can lose individual values and behaviors and instead adopt the flawed, assumptive, negative thinking of the group, inflating their unconditional bias and strengthening the drama triangles in place at work. Cliques end up reinforcing negative opinions and false assumptions about non-members. Those outside the clique become perceived as rivals, imbeciles, or threats.

Sadly, the formation of cliques in the workplace often begets more cliques. In an effort to survive, other employees band together socially to weather the drama created by others.

Bye-bye, teamwork. Hello, drama.

Perhaps that's what you're facing now: multiple cliques that have evolved into warring factions. Like the "race problem" group described in the introduction to this book, these groups ultimately reach the point where they discourage camaraderie across the whole team, preferring the comfort and security of a smaller, more isolated group.

If cliques are an active, corrosive presence in your workplace, there are several steps you can take to minimize their influence and, in some cases, abolish them entirely. If cliques have taken hold where you work, a key first step to disabling their power and influence is to remove any toxic personnel leading the cliques. As outlined in Part 1, many of the DDBs that drive drama, including gossip and cliquish behavior, are driven by actively disengaged employees. In some cases, the behavior of individuals and cliques, progresses beyond incivility to bullying. For an expert explanation of the differences between the two, see the Advice from an Expert in this section.

Advice from an Expert:
BULLYING VS. INCIVILITY
by Dr. Renee Thompson

I frequently get asked by organizations to help them eliminate workplace bullying. When I go in, I "pull back the covers and lift up the gown" to find out if there is really a bullying problem.

Sometimes I find bullying.

I almost always find incivility.

People tend to misunderstand the difference between bullying and incivility. Keep in mind: Both bullying and incivility are NOT okay. Both need to be addressed, but it is important to understand the differences, because the strategies to eliminate each are a bit different.

For a behavior to be considered bullying, it has to include 3 things: a target, harmful behavior, and repetition.

The target can be a single person or group of people. For example, a bully might pick on a single new hire or the group working on the opposite shift. The harm might be to the target ("I get diarrhea every time I have to work with her ...") or harmful to a customer (an employee who sabotages or sets up another for failure, affecting customer experience). Lastly, the behavior can't be just a one-time event. The harmful behavior has to be repeated over time. Some experts say 6 months or more. I disagree. I would consider a behavior as bullying if it occurs several times over the course of a week or so.

Incivility is different than bullying. While some behaviors can be similar, they tend to be lower level. Incivility often is behavior you might describe as rude or inconsiderate. Make no mistake, though: Incivility is a professional workplace killer if left unaddressed when it occurs.

Bullying, on the other hand, should be an event that NEVER occurs.

If you are truly experiencing bullying, there are several steps you can take to address your situation. First, get clear about the behavior and how it is impacting the work. Getting specific ("Jared called me an idiot in front of patients") can provide the opportunity to address specific behavior. Second, start a documentation trail of bullying behavior that includes dates, times, locations, incidents, witnesses, etc. Any time you can include verbatim comments, be sure to do so. And always link the bad behavior to a customer experience concern or strategic goal violation. Third, confront. One strategy is just naming the behavior, "You just called me in idiot in front of everyone," or "I just saw you roll your eyes at me." Simple confronting by naming behaviors in real time can start the process of eliminating bad behavior. While confronting doesn't always work, I guarantee that NOT confronting NEVER works!

Bullying and incivility can destroy your work environment AND impact those you serve in a negative way. The first step to addressing both is to get clear on the behavior – is it bullying (targeted, harmful, repeated) or incivility (low-level, rude, and unprofessional)?

Dr. Renee Thompson is the President and CEO of the Healthy Workforce Institute, which works with healthcare organizations that want to overcome the leadership and clinical challenges their people face every day. For more information, visit www.reneethompsonspeaks.com.

Another key action to disrupt cliques is the creation of workplace partnerships that force members of the clique to work with and get to know non-members, in settings unaccompanied by other members of the clique. This disturbs the us-against-them mentality. As they say, it's hard to hate someone up close. Over and above these one-to-one pairings, team leaders may need to periodically assemble the whole team for more intensive discussion of the dysfunction on the team. These kinds of "get-it-all-out-on-the-table" meetings often are uncomfortable and likely will require expert facilitation to be healthy interventions.

Of course, the best way to prevent the damage cliques cause is to prevent them from forming in the first place. Does that mean all members of a team have to be friends with everyone else on the team for that workgroup to succeed? Of course not. That's unrealistic. Differences in age, personality, race, culture, gender, stage of life, and more will influence the relationships people form in the workplace and will certainly result in some feeling a stronger, safer, more natural connection with others. Friendship between every single member of a team is not required to become a high-performing, low-drama team.

What is required are the very elements being explored in this book. Courtesy and respect, as outlined in Part 1, and camaraderie, as outlined in Part 2, go a long way to minimizing the formation of cliques. So, too, does disrupting the formation and perpetuation of the drama triangles present where you work.

How do team leaders go about tearing down drama triangles or, better yet, preventing them from forming in the first place? By prompting more careful and reflective thinking about others' motives and character, among all who make up the team.

BREAKING THE CYCLE OF UNHEALTHY CONFLICT

In our imagined scenario, outlined earlier, we made a snap judgment about the driver of the black four-door sedan who sped past you while you were stuck in traffic. That instant reaction assumed malice and poor character.

It probably never occurred to you that there might be a perfectly good explanation for his behavior. It didn't cross your mind that his behavior might actually be justified until a new piece of information was introduced: the "what if?"

I posed the question: What if I told you that seated next to the driver of that car was his wife, who is in labor, and they can see the baby's head?

I interrupted your natural predilection to assume character and judgment flaws in others with a piece of information designed to evoke empathy. I did this because I wanted to prompt more careful and reflective thinking. I wanted to present you with an alternate theory, one you might be sympathetic toward. Yes, it's possible the driver of the black four-door sedan is a horrible person, selfishly barreling his way through traffic, unconcerned with safety, manners, or laws. That could all be true.

Or he could be an otherwise reasonable, well-intentioned person. There actually could be a legitimate explanation for his behavior. I can land on that alternative theory quickly, a theory designed to challenge my bias, by asking a simple question:

What might make a good person act that way?

Team leaders can disrupt the flawed, egocentric thinking that drives drama by challenging team members to evaluate the range of motives other members of the team might have for their actions. Challenging team members to assume good intentions in others is a key tactic in the war against team drama. If you want team members to avoid jumping to the wrong conclusions about one another, you have to teach them to notice when they are assuming malice.

That kind of careful, reflective thinking is what made Officer Tony so good at his job.

Tony was a veteran officer on the police force at the large, public university where I held one of my first jobs. As part of my duties, I was responsible for serving in a monthly overnight on-call rotation on the weekends.

Trust me. If your job ever requires you to work an on-call nighttime weekend duty rotation on a college campus, you will most assuredly encounter drama. The combination of youth, alcohol, and risk-taking virtually guarantees it.

I hated that part of the job. When I was on duty, I spent considerable time witnessing the belligerent, immature, sometimes destructive behavior of impaired college students. The interactions my work forced me to have with these students regularly left me flummoxed and irritated.

But not Tony.

Tony not only kept his cool, but most of the time, he was downright jovial. No matter how abrasive or argumentative a student became, Tony was on his or her side. He ranged from kind and supportive to gregarious and chummy. And nothing about his nature was fake or contrived.

The students on that campus all knew Tony, and they adored him. Despite working the night shift most weekends for years, he still genuinely cared about each student, no matter how difficult or disrespectful. His approach never wavered, despite years being on the frontlines in a very tough job.

One Saturday night when I was on duty, Tony and I were involved in a particularly tense and exasperating encounter with a combative student. Afterward, I vented my frustration. "How do you do this every weekend?" I asked. "I can't stand coming out here even once a month. How do you stomach dealing with kids like that all the time?"

"Oh, that's easy," he said. "I'm seeing them on their worst day."

I was pretty young and clueless back then, which is probably a perfect description for the expression that crossed my face at his comment, so Tony continued.

"Look, let's be honest. If you're 18 and you're spending your Saturday night with me, that's probably your worst day. I'm not meeting you at your best. I'm not getting to see who you really are, your character, your true nature. I'm not getting to see you with your family or any good works you contribute to our community. No, it's pretty much a given that, most of the time, when I'm having contact with one of these students at night, I'm seeing them on their worst day. And I wouldn't want anyone to judge me based on my worst day, so I try not to judge them by theirs."

I've remembered that conversation for my entire adult life. It took place almost 25 years ago. To this day, I still find Tony's outlook inspiring.

Somewhere along the way, Tony chose to adopt a mindset that would minimize leveling harsh judgment on students' behavior. In fact, he adopted a belief system that ensured he would always remain supportive and empathetic toward others, no matter how he was treated.

He chose NOT to assume malice. Instead, he chose to believe that, in the face of appalling or thoughtless behavior, he was encountering a good person having a bad day.

This is the kind of thinking team leaders must promote among members of a team. When team leaders frequently remind employees to assume good intentions, they equip their teams with one of the critical thinking skills essential to preventing drama triangles.

To disrupt drama triangles and prevent webs of drama from forming, leaders must challenge flawed thinking and re-direct team members away from Victim and Rescuer behaviors. Leaders must help the Victim see that he or she is not helpless or being harmed, and that the Persecutor is probably not evil. Team leaders also must help the Rescuer learn that the healthiest response when approached by a Victim isn't to validate their victimhood, but to instead encourage them to go directly to the source of their anger or angst.

One way to advocate for these behaviors on your team is by inviting team members to have conversations together about how conflict will be handled when it arises. There may even be value in sharing the drama triangle with your team, including descriptions of each of the roles, and starting a discussion about when and where these patterns unfold where you work. From there, teams can begin identifying and adopting behaviors that allow conflict to unfold in a healthier way.

 Staff Conflict Agreement Facilitator's Guide. To download a facilitation guide for a staff activity that creates a consensus around how team members will handle conflict, visit **NoMoreTeamDrama.com.**

 ## Case Study:
The Boss's Angry Email

A few years ago, one of my clients, Angie, asked me to help her work out the best response to an angry email that one of her bosses, Dr. Laura, had sent to all the employees in the office. Dr. Laura had been growing frustrated with what she saw as inefficiencies and process-flaws in the office. Dr. Laura had been with the team for less than a year. She had been brought on as a new partner by the ownership group. That Monday, Dr. Laura's frustrations boiled over and she sent an email to everyone working there. Angie described that email, and its impact, in colorful terms.

"She bitched out the whole team over email. She just let everyone have it. Told them their approach was unacceptable. Questioned their commitment. Just assailed them."

"Have you had the chance to talk to anyone on your team about it? What kind of reaction are they having?" I asked.

"Yes, I've talked to a few. It's like a giant bomb went off. They're really angry. I don't know how they are going to stand working with her when she's back in the office on Wednesday."

"On a scale of 1-10, how angry are you about this email?" I asked.

"19," Angie replied.

"Okay," I said. "Here's what I suggest. Email or text her and just say, 'Something has happened as a result of this email that we need to talk about. What time can I call you tomorrow to fill you in?' This will buy you some time to get ahold of your own emotions."

I went on to tell Angie about the drama triangle. I explained that in this situation, Dr. Laura probably felt like a victim. She was assuming some things about the staff, whom she saw as persecutors, that were untrue or unfair. I also explained that, right now, the members of the staff undoubtedly feel like victims, with Dr. Laura as a persecutor. All conversations taking place between the members of the team were certainly validating their victimhood.

Afterward, Angie shared a powerful insight. "I understand where Dr. Laura is coming from. I know she's trying to improve our patient experience and our efficiency, but now everyone just feels attacked, disrespected, and unappreciated."

"You just described intent vs. impact," I told her. "That's going to be a key distinction to explore in your conversation with her."

"What should I say?" Angie asked.

"I can't tell you that," I answered, "because you know the players and the circumstances much better than I. But I can give you some food for thought."

"Okay."

"I want you think about the kind of conversation you need to have with Dr. Laura to disrupt her belief that she is a victim or that the staff are persecutors. I also want you to figure out a way to acknowledge any good intent she had with her email, but then help her see the actual impact it had, regardless of her intent."

Angie was quiet for a moment, then said, "Okay, I think I can do that."

Then I gave her a starter script.

"When you talk with her tomorrow, start out by saying, "Dr. Laura, help me understand what you hoped would happen as a result of the email you sent yesterday."

"Oh, I like that!" Angie remarked.

"Call me tomorrow after you talk to Dr. Laura and let me know how it went."

The next day, Angie filled me in.

"It was amazing, Joe. She had no idea her email was so nasty. When I asked her to describe what she hoped would happen, she said she was just trying to fix some issues. She wants people to pay more attention to the things she was asking for."

"What happened next?" I asked.

"I told her that I knew that's what she was going for, but that there was no way it would happen now because of the tone of her email. I told her the staff felt attacked and chewed out. At first, she kept coming back to her intent of trying to fix things, but eventually she admitted she could have handled it better."

"Did you explore any of the victim-persecutor stuff we talked about?"

"I tried. I just told her that the staff does a lot of things for her and for our patients that she doesn't see, and I that I wish she wouldn't assume that they aren't committed. I know that they are."

"That's very good, Angie. You directed her away from assuming malice. You tried reframing her view of the team as generally having good intentions. So how did you leave things?"

"She said she would be more careful about the tone of her emails, which is good, but I pushed and told her that I thought she needed to apologize to the staff. She finally agreed. I tried to get her to do it in person, but I think it will be another email."

"What are you going to do next?"

"I ... I don't know. I hadn't really thought about it."

I explained that an entirely different drama triangle was still in place. The one where the staff sees themselves as Victims and Dr. Laura as a Persecutor.

"Won't her apology help with that?" she asked.

"Maybe. For some. But do you think there are some folks on your team who will hold a grudge? Do you think some may brand her in a bad way for all time because of this, no matter what she says in the apology?"

"Probably!" she laughed. "Some of my girls are tough."

"Then after the apology, find a way to chat with the team. Ask them to decide whether Dr. Laura is a bad person or made a mistake. It's a way to steer them away from seeing her as evil to seeing her as *like them*."

In the days that followed, Angie pushed Dr. Laura to apologize. When she did, Angie followed up with her team, debriefing the whole experience with them and asking if they could forgive Dr. Laura. The results were overwhelmingly positive for everyone involved. Angie did what many team leaders avoid: She stepped into the discomfort of a confrontation. She also challenged the assumptions each party was making and pushed them to examine their own thoughts and behaviors. By doing so, she prevented what certainly would have become a long-simmering episode of anger and resentment between members of a team. Did drama occur in this scenario? Yes, but it was addressed quickly, handled openly and honestly, and the result – the healthy navigation of team conflict – ultimately made the team stronger.

When someone on the team lashes out or frustrates others, too many team leaders roll their eyes and say, "That's just the way she is. Try to ignore it." These teams are destined to suffer regularly with drama. When team leaders understand the root causes of drama (as you do now because you bought this book; congrats on that excellent decision, by the way), and are willing to be part of uncomfortable conversations to deconstruct it, drama is rendered far less injurious and contagious. Stop avoiding uncomfortable conversations. Stop prioritizing harmony over conflict. Otherwise, drama reigns.

A CHAT A DAY KEEPS THE DRAMA AWAY

If you want to guide your team toward consistently healthier responses to conflict (and thus reduce team drama), then you must have a variety of conversations with your personnel day to day. You will have to point out and affirm those behaviors that are key to healthy conflict, so that you are constantly reinforcing the very behavior you want to see consistently. You will have to help your team members understand the difference between intent and impact. This applies not just to any communication they initiate but to any feedback they receive as well. It also may be helpful to use an evidence-based personality assessment to give your team insights into some of the naturally occurring personality differences that exist within the group. Such an experience can help members better understand why others are the way they are while simultaneously giving each person specific ways to flex their own style to be more successful.

Some of those conversations will be about disrupting the assumptions employees make about others. When you hear a member of your team describe someone else in an unflattering way, challenge the characterization. Ask, "Why do you say that?" Ask, "What evidence do you have that that is accurate?" Tell them, "Okay, that might be true," then ask, "But what if it's not? What could be a perfectly good explanation for their behavior?" When you see an employee assuming malice or making up a story about another's motives, poke holes in the flawed thinking that you know is taking place. Point out where they may be more favorably judging themselves and more harshly judging others.

You also will have to have conversations that push employees to have their own uncomfortable conversations with each other. When an employee comes to you with a complaint about someone else, ask first if they've gone to that person directly. If the answer is no, challenge their reasoning. Ask them, "If someone on the team was frustrated with you, would you want their first step to be coming to me – your boss – or would you prefer they bring it to you first?" Most acknowledge that they'd prefer to be directly contacted. If your employee acknowledges this, point out that it's reasonable to assume their co-worker feels the same way. If your team has established this expectation as part of a staff agreement exercise, then invoke that expectation. Then pivot to helping the employee prepare for that conversation. Ask them to roleplay with you if necessary. Explain that while a peer-to-peer conversation might be uncomfortable, that's not a good enough reason to avoid it.

On top of these kinds of conversations, you also will have to teach your employees how to give and receive feedback. This involves giving employees tools and scripting for expressing their frustrations in a calm, non-accusatory manner. It involves talking through ways to react to feedback that stings or that is perceived as illegitimate in a courteous and respectful way. As you explore the various training and development needs of your team, keep these skills on your radar. They are key to keeping drama at bay.

GETTING BETTER AT CONFLICT

At the core of this section of the book is an examination of the predictable patterns of behavior that occur when employees jump to conclusions about their co-workers' motives and character. The strategies and tactics put forth to support healthy conflict and prevent unhealthy conflict are all rooted in empathy. That is, they are all ways to get your team members to re-evaluate their opinions of others and, hopefully, give them the benefit of the doubt more often. This is necessary to short-circuit the negative narratives we project onto others but never toward ourselves.

Despite all that I've outlined here, I must acknowledge that, every once in a while, we encounter someone on a team who will never show empathy toward a co-worker. Some will simply never engage in the kind of reflective thinking that disrupts the story they invent about someone else. No amount of coaching or counseling will get them to admit that the thinking behind their initial reaction was faulty or that their co-workers aren't wrong. From time to time, you will encounter someone who is so entrenched in their own victimhood in the workplace that it's impossible to shatter the drama triangle that exists around them.

When this occurs, we find ourselves forced to again label a member of the team as toxic. Their presence will continue to do harm for as long as they are allowed to remain on the team. There will be no courtesy and respect, no camaraderie, and no shift away from unhealthy conflict to the healthier kind. In this situation, we find ourselves once again in the unenviable position of having to remove someone from the team in order for that team to heal, grow, and improve. This must be acknowledged, because in a book designed to identify key tactics for reducing team drama, the act of removing a toxic employee is certainly crucial.

Beyond removing those who must go, a team leader who wants to get better at conflict must take responsibility for negating the impact of the flawed thinking that employees bring into the workplace. I know what you're thinking. Really? Is that really my job? In a perfect world, no, it wouldn't be. In a perfect world, team leaders would not have to take on the responsibility of nurturing higher-level critical thinking and conflict resolution skills among their employees.

But this isn't a perfect world.

This is a human world. And in this human world, your human employees enter your workplaces with unconscious biases. They bring with them assumptive, egocentric thinking that leads to predictable reactions, which creates drama.

If you want to achieve new results, then you cannot allow erroneous thinking and damaging behaviors.

Your team will get better at conflict when you help your employees become more thoughtful, reflective thinkers. They will get better at conflict if team leaders like you challenge their assumptions, summon their empathy, and teach them skills related to communication and conflict resolution. So work hard to spot drama triangles when they form (or even better, before), and when they do, intervene. Incite your team members to assume the best in each other. Encourage people to take responsibility for their actions on one of their, as Officer Tony might say, "worst days."

Otherwise, the members of your team are just waiting under a Disney Princesses pillow with the belief that they are hidden from drama.

But they're not.

Drama can see them. And it *will* find them.

KEY TAKEAWAYS
on CONFLICT for TEAM LEADERS

+ Conflict is integral to the growth and development of a team. Conflict, when healthy, draws out ideas, creates buy-in, and gives all members of the team a voice.

+ Healthy conflict occurs around ideas, assumes good intentions, is in service to your cause, and all exchanges are rooted in courtesy and respect.

+ Unhealthy conflict occurs in the shadows, assumes malice about people, typically includes DDBs, and often avoids direct discussion or honesty.

+ Because we are egocentric, we assign greater significance to our own beliefs, knowledge, and experience. We distort the level of our own stress and suffering.

+ At the core of almost all team drama is people reacting to how they perceive they were treated by others, but those perceptions often are inaccurate.

✦ Drama triangles form because it is easier to seek out the comfort of validation than it is to step in to the discomfort of confrontation.

✦ To disrupt drama triangles and prevent webs of drama from forming, leaders must challenge flawed thinking and redirect team members away from Victim and Rescuer behaviors.

KEY ACTION STEPS
on CONFLICT for TEAM LEADERS

✦ Remove any toxic personnel leading cliques or consistently engaging in any of the other DDBs outlined in Part 1.

✦ If cliques are present, create partnerships that force members of the clique to work with and get to know non-members, in settings unaccompanied by other members of the clique.

✦ Consider a get-it-all-out-on-the-table meeting, carefully facilitated, to helps teams get past established drama or long-standing issues.

✦ Challenge team members to assume good intentions in others. Help them notice when they are making up a story about another person's motives or character.

✦ Create a Staff Agreement about conflict that outlines a few guidelines, agreed to by everyone, for how members of the team will handle conflict when it arises.

✦ Encourage employees not to fear or avoid uncomfortable conversations. Role play with them to help them prepare as needed.

✦ Take responsibility for teaching members of your team how to give and receive feedback in clear, non-threatening ways.

Remember, to access the tools and videos discussed in this section, visit **NoMoreTeamDrama.com.**

PART IV

CAUSE

A common cause leads to interdependence
and shared effort.

CAUSE

When 10,000 adults in the United States were asked which company among the Fortune 500 they would most want to work for, the answers weren't surprising. The companies that topped the list all have reputations for being engaging places to work that offer unique benefits and environments to employees. Familiar names such as Google, Apple, Nike, and Delta Airlines all landed in the top 10. The top spot?

That went to the Walt Disney Company.

What makes an organization an appealing employer? Survey respondents were asked about reputation, trustworthiness, influence, and global impact, and in these areas, Disney outranks everyone. A closer look at Disney reveals that not only do people want to work there, but the people who already do, stay. Take, for example, the Walt Disney World Resort in Orlando, FL. Despite wages that rank as just average among travel industry companies, Disney boasts a below-average turnover rate. Why?

The difference is in the difference-making.

Disney World's new hire orientation program is two weeks long. That's right, there is a minimum of 10 full days of training before a new employee gets to step into his or her job or interact with a guest. That time is devoted to teaching new employees about Disney culture and having them complete

Disney communications training. This time also is spent helping all new employees understand the way Disney employees must show up to "create magical moments for guests of all ages."

That's the cause every employee and every team at Walt Disney World is charged to serve. If you know someone who has worked at any Disney property, that person will tell you that this cause – *create magical moments for guests of all ages* – is something that is talked about all the time, over and over.

New hire orientation at Walt Disney World introduces this big picture cause, and then spends time during the 10-day program sharing the little stories that illustrate this cause in action. One way they do this is with video interviews of guests. One notable video showcases a grandmother telling the interviewer about the birth of her grandson. Shortly after his birth, the proud grandma pulled her son aside and told him that she was going to save up and take the grandson to Disney World someday. As the camera pulls back, the employees in orientation see the young man standing next to his grandmother.

He is 12 years old.

It took the grandmother 12 years to save enough money to visit Disney World. She shares details in the video of the ways she saved a little bit of money, here and there, to make good on her promise. As the video ends, attendees are awash in emotion, thinking of their own grandmothers and marveling at the special effort made by the woman in the video. When the lights come up, the facilitator tells attendees the hard truth:

She is never coming back.

It took that grandma 12 years to save up enough money to visit for a few days. It's highly unlikely she will return to Disney World again. Orientation attendees are asked how knowing her story influences how they would interact with her. They are asked what kind of experience they want to create for her and her family. As you can imagine, the answers are boisterous, passionate, and filled with emotion. Participants describe their sincere desire to create an unforgettable experience and lifelong memory for that family. Then the facilitator makes the larger point.

That grandma is in our park *every single day.*

The orientation class nods in understanding. Their cause – to create magical experiences for guests of all ages – means more now.

WHY CAUSE MATTERS

Much has been written, both in academic research and in the hundreds of leadership books marketed by major publishers every year, about the power of purpose. Teams that are unified around a clear goal – a common cause – are more productive, have lower turnover, and are more likely to excel at customer satisfaction.

Purpose-driven teams also experience higher levels of group cohesion and lower levels of drama. When employees believe their work makes a difference in the lives of others, they are more likely to rise above petty disputes, remain resilient in the face of stress, and demonstrate a sense of team spirit. A common cause leads to interdependence and shared effort at work. Why? Because difference-making outranks drama.

You already know this, even if you don't know that you do.

Has your team ever overcome an unexpected disruption or obstacle? Has it ever come together to get through a challenging issue or difficult time? I bet it has. Maybe the group had to keep serving customers through a power failure or software crash. Perhaps your team experienced a series of cutbacks, layoffs, or call-offs, and had to fight through weeks of being stunningly understaffed. Or maybe your team endured a tragedy together, rallying in the face of heartbreak and pain.

The point is, you have seen a common cause in action. You have witnessed how the presence of a meaningful shared purpose led your team to rise above disagreements and stress. I'm willing to bet that on at least one day, your team showed you they are capable of ignoring or avoiding drama in service to something bigger.

In most cases, it takes some kind of pain or misfortune to trigger this group focus. What if, instead of relying on glitches, mayhem, or tragedies to jumpstart shared effort here and there, you could fuel that collaborative effort continuously, without needing trouble to cause the effect?

Since we know our teams are capable of rallying to a cause, and since we know that a cause is essential to team growth, doesn't it stand to reason that leaders at every level should learn how to champion a powerful purpose that stirs the souls of their personnel?

After years of training managers at all levels of leadership, I've become convinced that learning how to articulate a compelling cause for employees and learning how to constantly champion that to individuals and teams is an essential skill for any supervisor.

In this section of the book, we'll explore how to identify and articulate a common cause around which your team will rally. We also will identify specific strategies and tactics to introduce and continuously champion your cause to your team. To be successful, you will have to develop a skill that you have probably never thought of as essential for success as a team leader.

You will have to become a better storyteller.

TELL THE BIG STORY

If you've taken any kind of coursework on leadership, and specifically on improving team performance, you may have encountered Bruce Tuckman. More specifically, you've likely seen Tuckman's Model of Group Development. Published in 1965, it has been widely accepted as an elegant and helpful explanation of team development and behavior.

Tuckman's Team & Group Development Model

Tuckman suggests that teams evolve in stages. When teams first come together they are said to be *Forming*. In this stage, members of the team act as individuals and there is a lack of clarity about the team's purpose and individual roles.

Teams then proceed into a stage called *Storming*. In this stage, conflict arises as people begin to establish their places and debate the purpose and vision for the team. While some teams get through this stage quickly, and others avoid it altogether, approximately 50% of teams experience this stage of intragroup conflict. When they do, important guidance and skill-building from leaders (ahem, see parts 1 and 3 of this book …) are key to continued group progress.

If the team can successfully navigate and overcome the Storming stage, they will eventually move into the *Norming* stage. Teams in this stage acquire a level of consensus and agreement within the team. Clarity about individual responsibilities and the common goal emerges, with the leader having played a key role in promoting both the clarity and the consensus.

As time passes and the team progresses, they may eventually reach the highest level of team performance, the *Performing* stage. In this stage, the group has a clear strategy and shared vision. It can operate autonomously and resolve issues positively.

While Tuckman's model has been expanded and adapted since its initial publication, these four stages are foundational to nearly every version that has been published, cited, and leveraged for learning. I share it with you here not because you need to memorize it, but to instead emphasize two points essential to the development of any team.

Re-read the paragraphs above about these stages and notice what must occur for a team to progress from one stage to another. Do you see how critical a common cause is to the evolution of a team? In the *Forming* stage, there is a lack of clarity about the team's purpose. In the *Storming* stage, there is debate over purpose and vision. In the *Norming* stage, there is more clarity about the common goal. To reach the desirable *Performing* stage, the group must have a shared vision.

The words *goals, vision,* or *purpose* carry slightly different meanings, but thematically they are the same. They all refer to a common cause shared by a group, the presence of which is essential for the growth and development of a high-performing team.

Your cause, the one that will accelerate team growth and reduce drama in the workplace, is the story of the difference your employees make in the lives of others.

YOUR STORY IN A SENTENCE

One of my training clients is a thriving fertility clinic in the Northeast. In one of my earliest workshops with their leadership team, I challenged the leaders in the room to tell me about their powerful purpose – the difference they collectively make in the lives of others. "That's easy," the clinical manager told me. "We make babies!"

"That's not good enough," I replied.

Everyone in the room gasped. "WHAT? Why?!" one of the physicians asked incredulously.

"Because so do I!" I exclaimed.

Everyone laughed, and then the doctor said, "Well sure, but if you and your wife have trouble, that's when you come see us."

"Ah," I said with a smile. "Tell me more about that."

And so, the doctor did. With a great deal of empathy and compassion, she described what it's like to be a patient of theirs. She described all the heartbreak, frustration, and fear that a couple has endured before ever setting foot inside their practice. She acknowledged that a couple may be signing up for more of the same heartbreak, frustration, and fear just by becoming clients and going through treatment and procedures. And with tears in her eyes, the doctor described watching her couples get dragged to the precipice of giving up hope, wondering if something they've dreamed about for much of their lives was just not going to happen for them.

"And then suddenly it does," she said quietly, her warm smile conveying the deep caring she feels for her patients and their suffering.

"Don't you see?" I asked. "You don't 'make babies.'"

They watched me carefully.

"You make dreams come true."

For a moment, nobody moved. Then, as they looked at each other and their smiles widened, they enthusiastically agreed. They realized how a small change to the way they talk about their work – from "we make babies" to "we make dreams come true" – truly captured all that their clients face and all that their employees do for those clients.

Your cause is the one-sentence story of the difference your collective work makes in the lives of others. That one sentence must trigger empathy in all who work on your team. To be clear, your cause is not your slogan (McDonald's: "I'm lovin' it!") or your tagline (Nike: "Just Do It.") or even your marketing message (WalMart: "Save Money. Live Better").

Your cause is about how we impact *them*; the people we serve as our customers, day in and day out.

Some organizations have figured this out and actively promote a cause to go along with their organizational mission, vision, and values. Southwest Airlines is a great example. Southwest consistently ranks highest among airlines for both customer service and profitability from year to year. If you go to their website, you will see that they have a Mission ("… dedication to the highest quality of Customer Service delivered with a sense of warmth, friendliness, individual pride, and Company Spirit"), Vision (To become the world's most loved, most flown, and most profitable airline"), and Values (Safety and Reliability, Friendly Customer Service, Low Costs, etc.).

They also list their Purpose: "Connecting people to what's important in their lives."

This is the cause that leaders at Southwest Airlines champion to their employees and teams. That single sentence conjures up so many of the stories Southwest passengers can tell about where they are going and why. Southwest's purpose reminds their employees that they reunite lifelong friends, send weary business travelers home to their families, and rush loved ones to a hospital bedside in time to say goodbye.

The more specific and personal your team's cause, the more powerful it becomes. Your single sentence has to conjure up all the ways your employees either relieve suffering or impart joy.

Now, beware the nebulous, jargon-filled purpose statement. Too many organizations talk about their work with generic, buzz-word-filled mission statements. Target, for example, says their mission is "to make Target your preferred shopping destination in all channels by delivering outstanding value, continuous innovation and exceptional guest experiences."

That doesn't exactly make the hair on the back of your neck stand up, does it? Of course not. Because that sentence doesn't evoke how Target relieves suffering or imparts joy for its customers. Furthermore, if you go to Target's "Purpose & Beliefs" website, you get nine paragraphs of explanation. That's right, nine!

If Target wanted to come up with a single-sentence cause that inspires effort in their employees, they should ask their employees to share all the ways they make a difference in the lives of others. They should mine their workforce for specific examples and identify the patterns and themes that emerge. Those stories can then be compartmentalized into a single statement – like "we make dreams come true" for a fertility clinic – that reflects those real-world stories.

(Target, if you're reading this, I can help you. Call me.)

For example, consider the three nurse managers I met from a urogynecology clinic a few years ago. They were participants in a one-day leadership seminar I held in Cleveland on the role managers play in fostering employee engagement. During the portion of the workshop where attendees try to articulate the powerful purpose behind their work, these women struggled. Over and over, their efforts to construct a single sentence purpose ended up focusing on the symptoms and afflictions they see in their clinics each day. After several attempts, one of the nurse managers threw up her hands.

"I can't get romantic about bladder leakage, Joe," she proclaimed.

The room burst into laughter.

"Fair enough," I said, smiling. "But let's stop talking about illness or disorders. Instead, tell me what it's like to be a patient with such an affliction. What does that feel like, day in and day out?"

She spoke almost without thinking, because of what she sees every day at work. "Well, some of these women can't even leave their house. They have no freedom. And if they do, there's a real chance they'll find themselves in an embarrassing situation. It's really a dignity issue, too, for many of them."

"There it is," I said.

"What?" she replied.

"Go back to your clinic and tell everyone who works there that your work revolves around a simple cause: We give women their freedom and dignity back."

Emotion and relief exploded on her face. "Yes," she said. "That's it. That's exactly it. How did you do that?!"

"I didn't. You did. Those are your words, not mine."

THE DIFFERENCE IS DIFFERENCE-MAKING

I recognize that not every job can be romanticized. Not every task or duty or responsibility can be connected directly to life-changing outcomes like curing cancer or making dreams of starting a family come true. But I do believe it's possible to connect every job to making a difference in the lives of others, even in small ways.

Take, for example, a collections manager named Denise I met in Kentucky not long ago, during a conference where I was the keynote speaker. She asked me for help.

"I manage 24 employees who work denials for hospital billing. They make phone calls to insurance companies all day long or go online to their website. How do I talk about what my group does in a way that's powerful?"

"Well," I asked, "What's the benefit of their work to the hospital? What happens when your callers are successful?"

"The claims get paid and the Accounts Receivable goes down. The hospital earns more money," Denise replied.

"And what happens when the hospital's balance sheet is healthy? What are the results of having a healthier operating margin?"

"Management is happy. The VPs are happy." She smiled.

"Is that it?" I asked.

"Pretty much."

"Denise, if you look at things that way, and you allow your team to look at things that way, the work will never be more than arduous, cumbersome, and sometimes painful tasks. See the bigger picture."

I explained that when the operating margin is healthy, there are tons of benefits to the people who work there. Healthy revenue levels allow the hospital to hire more staff, which spreads the burden of the work across more people, which benefits everyone. So staffing is better. That's not all. Facilities are better. Merit increases are better. Equipment is refurbished or replaced more quickly. Better doctors get hired. Perks, benefits, employee development opportunities, and more all can be impacted.

"I guess that's true," she said, unconvinced. I pressed on.

I asked her to think of the benefits to patients and families when the operating margin is healthy. We talked about how, when patients and families encounter clinics or hospitals that are well staffed, they don't wait as long. They get more personal attention. The people taking care of them are less stressed. And because the personnel are better, the care is better. And if the facilities are better, the hospital can expand, or offer more services, saving patients time and reducing unnecessary extra trips. On top of that, more revenue in the pipeline means the facility is likely able to provide even more sick, charity, or supplement care for economically distressed or underserved families.

"Denise," I told her, "The work your team does directly impacts SO MUCH. If I were in charge there, I would be telling my team constantly that what we do here every day *creates a better care experience for patients, and a better workplace for every caregiver.*"

Advice from an Expert:
How to Get Employees
to Serve Customers
By Jeff Tobe

The first step to getting your employees to love serving your customers is to grant them influence over their touchpoints. A touchpoint is defined as "*any opportunity to influence the customer experience.*" Think about how many touchpoints your team or organization has in any given day. Your on-hold message is a touchpoint. The restroom in your office is a touchpoint. Your business cards and invoices are touchpoints.

Most businesses have hundreds of touchpoints in any given customer experience. Get your team together and have everyone identify their own touchpoints. Then, explore which touchpoints have the biggest impact on customers and invite your employees to share their ideas for ways to improve those touchpoints. This gets people engaged at a grassroots level, which is key to engaging employees. The more engaged people are internally, the better the customer experience externally.

Recently, I did an exercise with all of the employees of a company that processes milk. They prioritized their touchpoints, eventually identifying pick-up and delivery drivers as a key touchpoint.

I took the drivers aside and congratulated them on this. You should have seen their faces! I don't think anyone had ever acknowledged them in this way before. Then, I asked the six drivers, "*What's one thing you could do to TWEAK this one little touchpoint?*" One driver described a joke he shares with others when the tells them he works for a milk processer. "I wonder if we can use that somewhere in the company," he asked.

Now, on the back of all of the milk company's trucks, in bold letters, it says, "*In case of accident, please have cookies ready. Lots and lots of cookies!*"

How do you think that driver felt when his company acted on his idea? How do you think he feels about his work?

Imagine if you did this with all of your team. Invite your employees to identify their touchpoints and come up with small tweaks that could make them a little better for your customers. Not only can these changes greatly affect your customer experience, but empowering your employees in this way gets you one step closer to an engaged workforce.

Jeff Tobe, M.Ed, CSP, author of Coloring Outside the Lines, *helps organizations design the ideal customer experience by getting employees more engaged at what they do every day. For more information about Jeff, visit jefftobe.com.*

CHAMPIONING YOUR CAUSE

What's the cause where you work? What's the one-sentence powerful purpose you can champion? Start working now on a succinct statement that captures the difference your work makes in the lives of others. It may sound like an impractical exercise to come up with such a sentence, but it's a highly effective way to keep your story – your *cause* – at the heart of everything you do, and to reap the benefits of the presence of such a cause.

The goal is to construct a single sentence that is emotional, powerful, and triggers empathy. "We make dreams come true" is truly the cause every one of the employees at the fertility clinic serves when they come to work every day. And if I'm an employee there, knowing that on any given day I have the opportunity to bring that kind of joy to a family, well, that wins in comparison to the staff drama vying for my attention that morning.

Describing your team's work in crisp, emotional, evocative terms turns everyone's minds on and tunes them all in to the same radio station.

The shortest path to a powerful single-sentence cause that tells your story is to ask the members of your team for help. A simple 20- to 30-minute discussion can produce a powerful sentence that captures the imagination of your personnel.

 Visit **NoMoreTeamDrama.com** to download the book's resource kit, which includes an activity called Coming Up with Our Cause. It's a facilitator's guide for taking your team through a conversation to begin idea generating around your "big story" single-sentence cause.

It's not enough to come up with a powerful one-sentence cause that your employees embrace and feel in their bones. You have to champion that cause and that means finding ways to talk about it over and over. Explore ways to ensure your employees encounter reminders of your cause everywhere. Post your cause in backstage areas. Talk about it at meetings, on conference calls, during selection and onboarding, and as part of annual reviews. Your cause should be on the lips of everyone who works for you. They should get tired of hearing you say it.

But that's not all. Your single-sentence cause doesn't come to life for the women and men on your team unless they connect the specific tasks and responsibilities of their individual jobs to the specific differences they make in the lives of other individuals. It's not enough to champion your big picture, single-sentence story. You also must tell the little stories.

Little stories are the specific ways the work of an individual employee made a difference in the life of an individual customer or colleague. Where our big story cause is about how we impact them, the little stories are about how *I* impact *you*. These little stories not only further support the big picture cause you are working hard to promote. They help short-circuit the frustration, defensiveness, or irritation employees sometimes project onto customers.

Earlier in this book, we learned that each of us is hard-wired to more favorably judge ourselves and more harshly judge others. As a result, we quickly assume malice in others and see ourselves as victims. This happens every day, whether you're a front-line, customer-facing employee or a CEO. It's human nature.

While we've discussed how this phenomenon shows itself between employees on work teams, it also happens repeatedly between your employees and your customers. Any number of customer behaviors can trigger your employees to assume the worst about that customer. If they perceive customers as curt, late, pushy, loud, slow, or unprepared, your employees will make not-fully-formed snap judgments about those customers, consciously or unconsciously. Those judgments will influence their thinking and behavior. It doesn't matter if the customer is truly wronging your employee in some way or just creating a minor inconvenience or interruption. If, in any encounter, your employee perceives himself or herself as a victim and the customer a perpetrator (as we discussed in Part 3), then the level of service quality goes down.

Just as Part 3 of this book outlined the ways you must disrupt the false assumptions employees make about one another, you also must disrupt the false assumptions your employees make about your customers. If you can prompt more reflective thinking that leads employees to see customers as mostly well-intentioned people in need of their help, the employees' service quality will be higher, their stress and defensiveness will be lower, and there will be far less fuel for drama in the workplace.

Little stories, highlighted continuously, can do just that.

TELL THE LITTLE STORIES

"I want to make a video," I declared excitedly.

"Ok," my boss, Tim, replied.

Tim smiled and waited for me to go in to more detail. At the time, I was the head of training for the mammoth outpatient division of a nationally-ranked academic medical center. I was putting the finishing touches on a 12-workshop management training series for leaders in the division. Tim, my Vice President of Human Resources, had given me an enviable amount of autonomy to create and launch the program as I saw fit.

I launched into my pitch for a video designed to showcase the kinds of stories leaders need to tell employees about customers.

"One of our workshops is designed to help managers understand the kinds of conversations and messages they need to share with employees, day in and day out, to produce greater effort and commitment. As part of that session, I want to script and produce a video.

"You've heard that famous quote about always being nice to others because they are probably fighting battles we know nothing about?"

Tim nodded.

"I want the video to show those battles."

I plowed on enthusiastically.

"Here's my idea. The video opens with a front-desk worker at her station behind the window as a patient approaches. While they are talking, which we can't hear, a caption appears above the patient's head that says, 'She had to take 3 busses to be here today.' The camera then slowly passes this patient and we are in the waiting room where we see a mother trying to comfort a crying infant. Above the mother's head a caption fades in and says, 'She's only had 4 hours of sleep in the last 2 days.' Then, slowly, we pan over and see an elderly gentleman waiting, staring off into space. His caption fades in and it says, 'Just lost his wife of 50 years, who handled everything.'"

As I eagerly described my vision for the project, Tim smiled and nodded knowingly. After a few moments, he put his palm up.

"It's a great idea," he said. "There's just one problem. It's already been done."

"By who?!" I inquired.

"Chick-fil-A."

Tim turned to his computer and after a few keyboard clicks, turned his monitor toward me. I leaned forward as he clicked play on the YouTube video.

I watched the idea come to life exactly as I had imagined, but not in a waiting room. It was in a restaurant. The end result is a powerful, thoughtful video that reminds us that most every person we encounter is worthy of our respect and empathy.

When the video ended, I slumped back in my chair. "Damn," I said. "That's perfect."

When Chick-fil-A produced this video, it was not intended for external distribution. It was designed to be used as an internal employee training tool. Only when senior leaders began speaking at conferences and sharing it there did it become more widely known.

 To see Chick-fil-A's "Every Life Has a Story" video, visit **NoMoreTeamDrama.com**.

The leaders at Chick-fil-A know that working in fast food environments can be challenging. These enterprises experience high turnover and low wages, making it tough to establish a culture of service excellence. Chick-fil-A knows how important it is for their workforce to come to work armed with empathy. "Every Life Has a Story" allows leaders to facilitate a conversation with employees about what they see, and don't see, every day at work and how it might shape the ways employees show up.

In other words, Chick-fil-A uses this video to highlight the little stories of individual customers as a way to inspire a greater level of effort and service among its employees.

This approach, it turns out, is rooted in some pretty compelling social science research.

ONE OVER MANY

If you have graduated from a college or university, you've probably received a call from them. Usually that call comes in the early evening, just as you are sitting down to dinner.

Many universities run development call centers. The callers employed there dial up dozens of alumni during each shift and initiate friendly conversations in an effort to solicit donations to the university.

And when you get one of these calls at 6:15 p.m., the voice on the other end most often belongs to a student. In fact, staffing these development call centers with student workers is common practice for colleges and universities all over the country.

A few years ago, researchers at the University of Pennsylvania wanted to conduct a research study that examined motivation and effort in the workplace. They elected to use student workers employed in call centers to evaluate their methods and hypothesis. The study produced some interesting results that are relevant to us as we examine how to champion a cause that moves others to action. Here's what they did:

The researchers set up three groups, which we'll call A, B, & C. All three groups were made up of student workers employed in a university call center. All participants spent most of their time at work dialing for dollars.

Group A was asked to read stories before each shift. These stories were written by previous call center student workers describing in detail the benefits they gained from holding that job and attempting to do it well. For example, a member of Group A might be given a story from Janet who said that putting forth maximum effort in this job helped her learn how to overcome objections, taught her better time management skills, and put money in her pocket each month.

Group B also was asked to read stories before each shift. These stories, however, weren't from prior call center workers. Instead, these stories were written by the students who had benefited from the scholarship fund for which the student callers were raising money. So, members of this group might have read a story from Tim who shared that he was the first child in his family to attend and graduate from college. Tim might have explained that he majored in criminal justice and that the scholarship he received allowed him to realize his dream of becoming a police officer.

Group C was the control group. They took no additional action other than going to work and making their calls.

Can you guess which group had the highest level of performance? If you guessed B, you are correct. Group B not only outperformed Group A and C, they raised nearly twice as much money compared to Group A.

If you think that Group B was more successful because they were confronted with ways their efforts helped others, whereas Group A only heard about ways their efforts helped themselves, you are only partially correct.

More on this in a moment.

For now, think about the last time you needed an X-ray or an MRI. You probably lay on a cold table or in a whirring tube, waiting patiently for the pictures to be taken. After the appointment, your scans were sent over to a radiologist, who examined the scan closely, noted his or her findings, and passed it back to your physician.

In 2008, Dr. Yehonatan N. Turner had just begun his intern year as a radiologist in Israel. Almost immediately, he grew frustrated at feeling disconnected from the patients he was examining. To overcome this, he pretended that the patient behind every lab that came his way was his father.

This practice led him to a powerful idea. What if each scan came with a photo of the patient?

Dr. Turner wondered if it would impact the performance of the radiologists interacting with each lab, so he launched a compelling radiology research study in which a photograph was attached to each patient's file. After three months, the radiologists participating in the study reported overwhelmingly positive results. They expressed feeling more connected to patients, being more attentive, and experiencing more empathy. They liked having the photos on the files, they declared, and thought it should continue.

But it's what happened next that's even more compelling.

The occurrence of incidental findings among the patients with photographs on their files was higher than normal. If you are not familiar with the term, an incidental finding is when the examining radiologist finds something he or she was not looking for. For example, a radiologist might be examining a knee ligament to determine if a tear is present and notice a bone cyst farther down the leg. That's an incidental finding. Among the pool of patients with photos on their files, more incidental findings were noted than were typical.

So, Dr. Turner extended his study. This time, he took all the photos off of the patient files and sent those same patient labs back to the radiologists. Consequently, the occurrence of incidental findings was much lower.

In fact, 80% of the incidental findings that were noted in the initial round of examinations were missed the second time around.

This stunning result confirmed what Dr. Turner had assumed all along. Feeling a personal connection to a patient isn't just emotionally satisfying for the physician. It actually makes the physician more effective.

The study of the student employees in the call centers and the study of the radiology labs with patient pictures share something in common. Both studies make it clear that if you want to use difference-making to inspire effort, you must connect personnel to one person specifically. You cannot simply talk about your clientele in general, as many organizations often do. Key to inspiring higher levels of effort is creating a line of sight between the work of individual employees and the ways it makes a difference in the lives of singular people.

We have to tell the little stories.

When you discuss why certain processes or employee behaviors are important in your workplace, you are probably discussing their impact on your customer population in general. You probably refer to *our patients, our guests,* or *our customers.* It's likely you discuss these groups as *groups,* and the terms you use to describe them are plural.

It would probably feel strange to announce that you are changing your operating hours to better accommodate "Mrs. Jones."

But it turns out that this kind of specificity is exactly what moves people to action.

This is the key insight offered in both of the research studies noted above. The student callers working the phones to raise money for a scholarship fund performed at a higher level when they were mentally pushed past thinking of the beneficiaries of the scholarship in general terms ("students"). It was only when they saw a direct connection between their efforts and a *specific person* that their performance increased. The same is true of the radiologists in Dr. Turner's study. When those professionals connected their efforts to an individual, they were more attentive and effective.

The lesson here is clear: As leaders, we have to tell stories about the differences our team members make in the lives of *individual people.* Need a few volunteers to take on extra work in the form of a committee-driven project? Be specific about how that committee's work will impact "Mary, Alanna, and George over in Purchasing." Trying to convince a Senior VP to greenlight funding for expensive new equipment? Share a precise example of how that new equipment ends suffering for a specific customer or employee.

Whatever new behavior or mindset you are advocating for, the key here is to position your employee as a hero. Find a way to create line of sight between their actions and the way it truly benefits another specific person.

In other words: Give them capes.

Leaders who go to work every day and convince their employees that they are heroes, rescuing individuals from pain and suffering, or bestowing happiness or much-needed assistance, get teams that want to perform. This approach moves people's mindset from "have to" to "want to" in the workplace. If I have to stay late to accommodate a last-minute order or customer visit, what determines whether I'm irritated by that development? What determines whether that irritation becomes obvious during a customer interaction? Typically, it's the difference between believing that I, as the employee, am being victimized by an inconsiderate customer or demanding boss, or believing that my help is truly needed. The story of the circumstance – real or imagined – determines my attitude. If I don't have the little story – the details of the circumstances of the client – then my focus will be on the inconvenience. It will be on my unhappiness, and I will see myself as a victim.

CASE STUDY:
FROM ANNOYED TO TRYING

Imagine for a moment that I work in a bakery. We've got about an hour left in our workday. We've completed all our baking for the day. I've already washed and put away all the supplies and equipment. The only thing left to do is finish working the front counter for customers who stop by to purchase off-the-shelf items. I'm looking forward to calling it a day, because after work I'm going to stop by my niece's t-ball game to watch her play. She's excited that her uncle is coming to her game.

Now imagine that moments later, my boss hangs up the phone, walks over to me and says, "Hey a late cake order just came in. *They need it in 90 minutes and I said we could do it. I need you to put this together now, please*," as he hands me a slip of paper with the details.

Imagine how I'm feeling about this development. If you guessed "annoyed," you're right. Should I make the cake and do it well because my boss told me to? Of course. But what might my attitude be as I go about the task at hand? Will the quality of my work product be impacted by those feelings? What do you imagine is my attitude about the customer? The answers to all of these questions are likely things you would want to avoid in your employees.

Had the bakery manager altered his or her approach slightly, connecting the action requested to the difference it will make to another person, it probably would produce an entirely different result.

Here's what the bakery manager might have said:

> *"So here's the story: I just got off the phone with a gentleman who bought a cake elsewhere for his daughter's birthday party this evening. He just got home and when he went to carry it inside, he dropped it. Right in front of his daughter. It's completely wrecked. This poor guy ... I could hear his daughter crying in the background. He asked if there's any way we can help them out. I told him I thought we could. The daughter's name is Layla, she's turning 7, and she loves 'My Little Pony.' So, what do you say? Want to be a hero?"*

Knowing the story, how might I feel about the task at hand now? Do you think that I might want to take this on, instead feeling that I have to? Might I be okay with calling my sister to tell her that I am going to be a few minutes late to the t-ball game?

I say yes, and I believe that's the case for most people. By telling me the story of the individuals involved in the situation, my boss would tap into my empathy. I'm more likely to personalize the circumstances and behave in a way that aligns with what I'd want others to do for me. Even if I'm only slightly impacted by the story of the dad and the cake drop, any incremental impact in my attitude or performance is still an improvement from how I would have shown up otherwise. In this example, my boss's effort to tell me the little story moved me away from annoyance toward genuine effort.

SYNTHESIZING YOUR STORIES

As we've discussed to this point, teams evolve in predictable stages. One of the most powerful catalysts for propelling teams from stage to stage is a shared purpose. If you want your team to evolve past the stages where drama is at its most prevalent and into the stage where it's fully minimized, promoting a common cause is key. The ways in which you talk about that cause have to be succinct – a single sentence that describes how the team makes a difference in the lives of others. That description is most effective when it highlights the ways your team's work relieves suffering or imparts joy. To champion that cause, employees must hear that big story message constantly while also hearing the little stories that specifically detail the ways their individual work benefits individual people.

Think back to the first real job you ever had. Many of our first jobs required effort but perhaps didn't always require a lot of intellectual energy. And at 16 or 17 or 18, you probably didn't naturally arrive to work with a zealous devotion to customer service. If we apply all the lessons about identifying and championing a cause as outlined in this section of the book, what might your experience have looked like? If you'll indulge me, let's use one of those "first jobs" to apply what we've explored here together. To make things interesting, let's pick a job with a fairly mundane, routine, at times even mindless set of responsibilities:

Ticket-taker at your local movie theatre.

You know the job I'm talking about, right? This is the teenager hired to stand at that tall ticket box next to a velvet rope and stanchion for hours at a time. His or her duties primarily involve looking at a ticket for the theatre number, tearing the stub in half, then telling customers over and over again "on your left" or "on your right." Not a real sophisticated gig, right? What is the difference he or she makes in the lives of others?

Not much, you might say.

I disagree.

If I were running a movie theatre and hired you for this job, I'd need you to believe that what you do for me at my movie theater is actually much more sophisticated than that. Because that's the only way I'm going to get you to try when you're tired. Or get you to come to work when you'd rather not. Or get you to, at a minimum, just bring a higher-quality energy to the interactions you have with those around you.

To get you to show up this way, I'm going to work to demonstrate that you, dear ticket-taker, are in the unique position of getting to be a part of a special occasion for almost every person that walks past you, every single day, while you are working.

Very early on in your tenure, I'm going to tell you that what we do here is help our customers escape stress, make memories, and have fun. That's my big picture cause. You are going to hear me say that constantly. And I'm going to do all that I can to make sure you see and hear specific examples of this. In other words, I'm going to share little stories, too. These are specific examples of how your work or our theatre makes a difference in the lives of others.

I'm going to point out when I see a father taking his young son to his first Star Wars movie, and then I'll ask you about the first movie you remember seeing as a kid. I'm going to direct your attention to the obvious excitement of those folks who line up early, in costume, for the latest superhero movie, and I'll ask you about the movies you were most excited to see over the course of your life. I'll also make sure you notice how affected and emotional our guests are after walking out of the latest Oscar-nominated tear jerker, and I'll ask you about the most recent movie you saw that made you cry.

Along the way, I'm going to answer any question you ask about "why" a rule is in place or a change is occurring not by citing policy, regulations, or organizational directives, but by telling you the story of how the policy, regulation, directive, or change impacts real people. I will find a way to connect my answer to your question to our larger cause of helping our customers escape stress, make memories, and have fun.

Then, not long after you've started working, I'll give you a fun piece of homework.

I'll ask you to get in touch with a couple you know who have been together longer than anyone else you know. Your assignment will be to ask them about their first date. Your homework will be to come back and tell me as much as you can about that first date of theirs.

After you tell me the details of the first date you learned about, I'm going to ask you a question. "Isn't it remarkable that they can remember so many details about a night that happened so many years ago?" Then, I'm going to make the point that this entire exercise built up to: "Guess what? Every single person walking past you while you take tickets might be in the middle of a night they'll remember for the rest of their lives. And we get to be a part of that! Isn't that something?"

After this conversation, I will probably wait a few weeks, then give you another assignment. I will ask you if you know anyone with children under the age of 8 and encourage you to ask them when the last time was that they went to a movie without the kids in tow. I also will suggest that you ask them what kind of arrangements they had to make to get away for a few hours. There's a pretty good chance you'll come back and tell me what most young parents already know. It's tough to get out to see a movie alone, and when they do get the opportunity, they have to pay a babysitter, leave detailed instructions, etc.

Why will I send you to talk to young parents? Because it drives home a key point that I want you to keep in mind while standing at the ticket-tearing station: Every person walking past you might be someone who had to arrange quite a lot just to get to our building tonight.

I will tell little stories over and over until you can't help but start to pick them out yourself. I want you play a small part in something that might be the thing our guests have been looking forward to all day or all week, or in the case of those anticipated new movies, months. And sometimes, we are the thing they remember for years.

GETTING BETTER AT CAUSE

The big stories and little stories advocated for in this section of the book act as food for your employees' souls. A common cause creates an energy that is powerful for both employees and customers, and it creates a culture in which people love to work. A common cause also is the essential ingredient that advances employees beyond having a relationship with their work that is entirely transactional.

Recognize that each of the employees discussed in this section of the book, despite impacting different people in different ways, are alike. Whether they work for a theme park, an airline, a doctor's office, a collections company, or a movie theatre, each of them is essential to an entire experience that makes a difference in the lives of others. The work of the ticket-taker at the movies is just as important as the work of a doctor in a fertility clinic or the work of a ride attendant at Disney World. The only difference between them is whether they've come to believe that their work is truly impactful. If they have, it's because of what they are told at work about what they do and how they matter.

If you want your team to focus, rally, and collaborate despite disagreement, you must deploy a continuous drip-drip-drip of messaging about the team's cause. This steady drumbeat of stories must come in the form of the big-picture difference your team makes in the lives of others and the little ways each person is a hero to individuals from day to day. When team leaders champion a cause that stirs the soul, something both emotional and tangible, the work becomes so worthy of a team's time, attention, and effort, that they can't help but rise above drama.

KEY TAKEAWAYS
on CAUSE for TEAM LEADERS

- ✦ Teams evolve in stages over time and key to that evolution is a unifying cause.
- ✦ Unity around a common purpose leads to more productivity, lower turnover, and better customer service.

✦ Your cause is made up of a single "big story" and a multitude of "little stories."

✦ The big story should focus on the ways your team, as a whole, relieves suffering or imparts joy.

✦ The little stories that most successfully connect people to a cause are the ones that describe the difference an individual employee made in the life of another singular individual.

✦ Leaders who convince their employees that they are heroes get teams that want to perform and that rise above drama.

KEY ACTION STEPS
on CAUSE for TEAM LEADERS

✦ Describe the ways the work of your team either relieves suffering or imparts joy.

✦ Work with your team to come up with a single sentence that acts as a suitcase packed full of the stories about the difference they make in the lives of others.

✦ Talk about your big-picture cause over and over. Post your cause in backstage areas. Talk about it at meetings, on conference calls, during selection and onboarding, and as part of annual reviews.

✦ Describe how the specific tasks and responsibilities of someone's job make a difference to others. Make them the hero of the story.

✦ Answer questions about "why" not by citing policy, regulations, or organizational directives, buy by telling the story of how the policy, regulation, or directive impacts real people.

✦ Plan and execute a steady drip-drip-drip of messaging about the team's cause.

Remember, to access the tools and videos discussed in this section, visit **NoMoreTeamDrama.com**.

EPILOGUE

EPILOGUE

Yes, it is possible. You CAN take a group of co-workers currently experiencing drama and transform them into a band of collaborators who reject drama in all its forms.

It is possible.

That doesn't mean that it's easy.

In the aftermath of learning about the impact Courtesy, Camaraderie, Conflict, and Cause can have on team drama, I hope it's clear that if you are a team leader, these things are part of your job.

Like it or not.

If you don't want to attack team drama by challenging your team to get better at Courtesy, Camaraderie, Conflict, and Cause, I strongly encourage you to go do something else. Otherwise, if you stay, you will preside over a team whose relationship with their work and each other will remain entirely transactional. You will end up cultivating a group where individuals focus on protecting their own self-interests. Many of your employees will never progress beyond doing the minimum in their jobs.

You also will regularly be confronted with drama and all of its consequences.

But if you've read this far and decided that you are ready to tackle drama, let me encourage you. Yes, it takes time and effort, but that doesn't mean you won't start to see results quickly.

Where should you start?

That depends on the dynamics of your team, the level of tension, division, and suffering that is currently taking place, and the degree to which you can truly influence that team.

As noted in the introduction, starting with Courtesy almost always is the right answer. Remember, the quality of interactions on your team is determined by what you expect and permit. Insist that members of your team treat each other with courtesy and respect at all times. Nurture that expectation while setting ground rules and championing your values all year long. Remove those toxic employees who create and thrive on drama and who don't change, despite being given every opportunity to do so.

If you've elected to start with Camaraderie, then work to enhance familiarity, connection, and bonds of belonging to propel your team forward. Decrease the distance between co-workers by giving them opportunities to get to know each other beyond the tasks and responsibilities of their job roles. Foster a sense of belonging by celebrating the team as a whole and by reminding members of the contributions of each member.

If unhealthy Conflict is your biggest problem, then drive your team away from the patterns of behavior that provoke unhealthy conflict and toward the kind of healthy conflict that helps teams reach the highest levels of performance. Help the members of your team see that the conclusions they make about others' motives and character often are skewed and incorrect. Teach them the communication skills they need to give and receive feedback more effectively.

And if your team is lacking interdependence and shared effort, identify a common Cause so worthy of their time, effort, and attention, that they can't help but rise above the petty drama that pops up in the workplace from time to time. Tell the big story of the difference your work makes in the lives of others and support it with the little stories about the ways your team members relieve suffering or impart joy.

Still not sure where to start? Then be sure to download the No More Team Drama toolkit and use the enclosed Team Drama Evaluation to examine the type of drama that is prevalent where you work. Use the questions and answers on this assessment to help you determine which of the four C's is most in need of your attention.

Also, be sure to ask yourself key questions and think through answers before diving into drama-proofing your team. What is your biggest obstacle when it comes to affecting change where you work? Perhaps the better question is: Who is your biggest obstacle? Is there someone on your team or in your organization who will be most resistant to your efforts? Can you make them an ally? Can you give them this book? Can you create line of sight between the pain of the drama that is taking place where you work and the ways it negatively impacts what is most important to them?

Also consider: What kinds of resources will you need to put the contents of this book into action? What kinds of conversations will you need to have? What kinds of training do you need? What kinds of training does your team need? What projects or tasks must you tackle right now to set yourself up for success?

Putting this book into action can be done in a variety of ways. You can simply use the Action Items at the end of this section to give you a set of tangible, real-world tasks to employ.

You can try focusing on one of the C's each quarter. Q1 can be Courtesy. Build a calendar and a set of team development experiences around those actions we outlined in the section on Courtesy. Then take a similar approach with Camaraderie in Q2, Conflict in Q3, and Cause in Q4.

If you want to cover more ground in a shorter amount of time, try dividing the year into thirds and work on a different C each month. Like this:

January: Courtesy

February: Camaraderie

March: Conflict

April: Cause

May: Courtesy

June: Camaraderie

July: Conflict

August: Cause

September: Courtesy

October: Camaraderie

November: Conflict

December: Cause

Or, you can simply pick one area to work on indefinitely until you see progress and results. Or take ONE action item from EACH of the four areas – Courtesy, Camaraderie, Conflict, and Cause – that you will work to consistently improve on your team over a defined period of time, say 3 months.

However you decide to start, commit to becoming a champion of a no-drama workplace. Make Courtesy, Camaraderie, Conflict, and Cause shared values across your team. In order for something to become a shared value, it must become more important than individual comfort, so encourage your employees to do what is hard when working with others. Drive them toward the uncomfortable conversations that must happen on the job, between team members, to ensure a no-drama workplace. Many of the things in this book are hard to do. Remind your personnel that the wrong choices are almost always the easiest ones to make.

Imagine where your team will be a year from now if you commit to this today. Imagine the problems you will prevent – that will never occur – because you decided right now, today, to take your team to a better place.

Imagine the drama you'll derail and never have to deal with if you begin working on Courtesy, Camaraderie, Conflict, and Cause right away.

You can do this. Truly, you can.

It is not easy, but it's also not complicated, if you trust the process.

Wherever you decide to start, remember this: There may be a corporate brand or owner's name on the front door of your office, but that is YOUR team in there. Own the culture that exists around that team. Insist on Courtesy. Commit to Camaraderie. Tackle Conflict. Campaign for Cause.

Talk with your team about drama. Ask more of them. Challenge them. Advocate for them. Care deeply about them. Become the gatekeeper that protects them and the environment they work in by being oh-so-careful about whom you allow to join and whom you allow to stay.

And decide right now, today, that drama will no longer be allowed to suffocate the effort and the spirit or your team. Decide right now, today, that drama will be beaten back by the collective efforts of you and your team members, who will commit together to creating a workplace worthy of them and a team they are proud to call their own.

You can do it. I know you can do it.

Now go get started.

ACKNOWLEDGEMENTS

Writing a book can be an incredibly gratifying experience. This is my second book, and I will admit that during the researching, mapping, writing, and editing of this book, I enjoyed bursts of satisfaction and fulfillment.

But most of the time, it was just hard.

I can't speak for other authors, but for me writing a book – a truly good book, one that is worthy of you, the reader, and that I am proud to adorn with my name – is painful. It's an intellectually exhausting exercise that requires loads of time and focus, two resources of which I am often in short supply. This is just my second book and it was as challenging as the first. Thankfully, I was blessed to have a number of incredible people supporting and advising me throughout the project.

Melissa Farr handled the layout and design of the book and did a stellar job. She also designed that fantastic cover you've been staring at this whole time. I'm madly in love with it. Thank you for your patience and flexibility, Melissa.

My copy editor Meagan Welling is a rock star. On this project, her attention to detail, amazing responsiveness, and genuine enthusiasm were invaluable. I'm lucky to have you on my team, Meagan. Thank you.

This book would not exist without my editor and coach Bonnie Budzowski. She lent her expertise and support to this project from concept to completion. The prose on these pages is tighter, clearer, and more useable because of Bonnie. Thanks for pushing me to further develop key ideas and making me coherent from page 1 (I think). You are a wonderful coach and an even better person. I'm privileged to know you.

Renee, Vicki, MJ, Kathy, Jeff, and Cara: From sharing your content and expertise to cheering me on along the way, you each contributed greatly to the quality and production of this book. It would likely still be on the "to-do" list were it not for your contributions and encouragement. I'm so lucky to call each of you colleagues and friends.

My deepest thanks also to my incredible family. My parents and in-laws are unflinchingly generous when it comes to being there to help amid our crazy schedules. You are all invaluable. Nothing that has happened in recent years would have been possible without your love, support, and constant willingness to pitch in. Thank you.

Finally, my most profound thanks go out to my incredible wife Jessica and our three beautiful children. Despite the constant travel this job requires, you selflessly supported me every time I had to steal away to keep this book moving forward. Of all the things I'm proud of in this life, our family tops the list. I love you all so very much.

Would you like Joe Mull to present
NO MORE TEAM DRAMA
at your next conference, meeting, or leadership retreat?

Do you want your next on-site training or keynote speaker to avoid reductive leadership **mumbo-jumbo and give your audience reality-based tactics and** answers they can **immediately apply** back in the workplace? Do you want your audience to be **captivated, entertained**, and **energized** by your presenter? If you answered yes to these questions, then Joe Mull is the perfect choice to be your speaker.

Joe doesn't talk about leadership in generic nuggets of fortune-cookie wisdom. He helps audiences tackle **the real stuff**: gossip, in-fighting, cliques, employees who say "that's not my job" or who "keep score," and more. His **laugh-out-loud funny** exploration of these issues along with his commitment to giving managers professionals **practical, actionable, real-world strategies** they can use the next day, make him a huge hit at conferences, meetings, retreats, and events.

For information about booking Joe as a trainer, meeting facilitator, or keynote speaker, visit **www.JoeMull.com**.

www.**NoMoreTeamDrama**.com

Made in the USA
Lexington, KY
16 July 2018